W9-BLO-188

STANTON PEELE, Ph.D. in social psychology at the University of Michigan, is a faculty member of the Department of Health, Teachers College, Columbia University. He has been investigating the phenomenon of addiction for nearly a decade and has written and spoken widely about the sources of addiction in our society and how people may resist them. He is the author of *Love and Addiction* (Signet, 1976).

STANTON PEELE

How much is too MUCH

Healthy habits or destructive addictions

PRENTICE-HALL, INC., Englewood Cliffs, New Jersey 07632

Library of Congress Cataloging in Publication Data

Peele, Stanton.
How much is too much.

(A Spectrum Book)
Bibliography: p.
Includes index.
1. Drug abuse. 2. Habit. 3. Health.
4. Mental health. I. Title.
RC564.P44 613.8 80-25630
ISBN 0-13-424192-4
ISBN 0-13-424184-3 (pbk.)

A SPECTRUM BOOK

10 9 8 7 6 5 4 3 2 1

Printed in the United States of America

Prentice-Hall International, Inc., *London*
Prentice-Hall of Australia Pty. Limited, *Sydney*
Prentice-Hall of Canada, Ltd., *Toronto*
Prentice-Hall of India Private Limited, *New Delhi*
Prentice-Hall of Japan, Inc., *Tokyo*
Prentice-Hall of Southeast Asia Pte. Ltd., *Singapore*
Whitehall Books Limited, *Wellington, New Zealand*

Contents

11 **The nonaddicted lifestyle** Balance and proportion 122

Preface

How Much Is Too Much tells us when habits become addictions. Because we incorrectly believe that addiction occurs only with narcotics, we often fail to identify our addictions. We may even mistake them for healthy habits. The criteria for addiction in this book indicate which are which, and how to keep our habits healthy.

Addiction is not an alien force which attacks us and our children from the outside. It is an expression of our way of experiencing life and of looking at such daily events as challenge and pain. Thinking of addiction as something we do to ourselves may make it seem doubly depressing. Actually, this book gives us the hope that our habits are manageable, and that nothing we wish to eliminate from our lives need harm us.

The addictive urges we feel grow from a number of past and present sources, many of them beyond our control. These include forces from the society around us—in advertising, in the media, in the organizations where we go to school and work. Recognizing how institutions affect us addictively may not mean we can modify society, but it at least gives us the chance to combat these pressures.

At the same time, we must be conscious of how our children are being shaped—both by social forces and forces within the home—in regard to addiction. We will find that attitudes and experiences at home are the best antidotes to the epidemic of alcohol and pill addiction among the young that we are so alarmed about.

The concept of habit is a useful one for working on our addictions. First, it helps us to realize that addiction is a habit gone out of control. Second, we can take advantage of the vast amount of research that has been done on habit modification. The technology of habit modification can show us how to change habits that trouble us before they grow to oversized proportions. If we have reached the point of genuine addiction, then we may chose to employ this technology within a therapy program. However, escaping addiction is more than modifying habits—it means changing the nature of our relationship to the world.

Obviously, there are things we do regularly which are good for us, and which thus form the basis of healthy habits. Not the mislabelled negative addiction I referred to, but habits which encourage our growth, our belief in ourselves, and the richness of our lives. Where do they come from and how do we get them? Perhaps most difficult—how do we keep them healthy rather than dissipating them or turning them into replicas of the addictions we wish them to replace? These are the questions we must constantly consider as we strive to balance our lives.

STANTON PEELE

Acknowledgments

I would like to thank Mary Arnold, Archie Brodsky, Donna Gertler, Paula Ives, and Cissy Schmidt for their help in preparing this book.

1
The addiction experience

When most of us think of addiction, we imagine a drug-hungry psychopath frantically trying to score some smack. We envision this person robbing someone to get money, meeting surreptitiously with a pusher, or going through the agony of withdrawal if he cannot locate a source of heroin or some other addictive drug. This image is incorrect in every particular. For example, many—if not most—of the people who take heroin can go through voluntary periods of abstinence, or switch to some other drug—such as alcohol, tranquilizers, or barbiturates—when heroin is not available.

It is important for us to recognize the facts about drugs and addiction so that we realize that addiction is not a distant phenomenon which affects only a few criminals. It is something that is as likely to occur with a perfectly presentable middle-class person as it is with a resident of the ghetto.

Consider the following descriptions of drug use: "[The user] is tremulous and loses his self-command; he is subject to fits of agitation and depression. He has a haggard appearance . . . As with other such agents, a renewed dose of the poison gives temporary relief, but at the cost of future misery." This is the medical view of the effects of coffee in England around 1900. Today, researchers have discovered the existence of withdrawal among regular users of cigarettes and coffee. People who rely on coffee to "perk them up" show the same array of symptoms when they fail to receive caffeine—headache, irritability, an inability to work effectively, nervousness, restlessness, and lethargy—as do narcotics addicts who go through withdrawal.

What does all this tell us about addiction? It indicates that addiction does not come from any one drug, nor is it the inevitable result of using any drug. Instead, addiction is something that may—or may not—be present for a user of any substance. It is this which points to the ultimate truth of addiction—it is not a drug problem at all, but a problem that people have. In some cases, it may not even involve the use of a drug. Drug addiction is based on the experience a drug gives a person and the place this experience has in the person's life. Anything that produces a comparable experience can likewise be addictive.

the addiction cycle

The experience most readily associated with addiction is the experience of oblivion, the erasing of consciousness. The drugs that are most often the objects of addictions—heroin and other narcotics, barbiturates, and alcohol—are drugs that diminish people's awareness. Pharmacologically, these drugs are classified as *depressants*. All of them are analgesics or painkillers. People turn to such drugs to get rid of uncomfortable feelings they have about themselves or their environments. Thinking about their lives causes them pain. Turning to the analgesic drug experience eliminates this pain, but it also lessens their ability to deal with the things that trouble them. The addiction cycle in Figure 1.1 is then completed. As the problems of the drug users worsen, their need for oblivion and an escape from pain increases.

The problems that trigger and result from the addiction cycle can be interpersonal, professional, or existential. For example, if a person needs money and is worried about losing his job and takes a drug to forget his worries, he exacerbates his problems first by spending money for the drug and then by incapacitating himself for work. Similarly, if a man is having trouble at home and goes out drinking to forget his problems,

figure 1.1.
The Addiction Cycle.
Addiction is a damaging cycle of behavior that feeds on itself and grows beyond control.

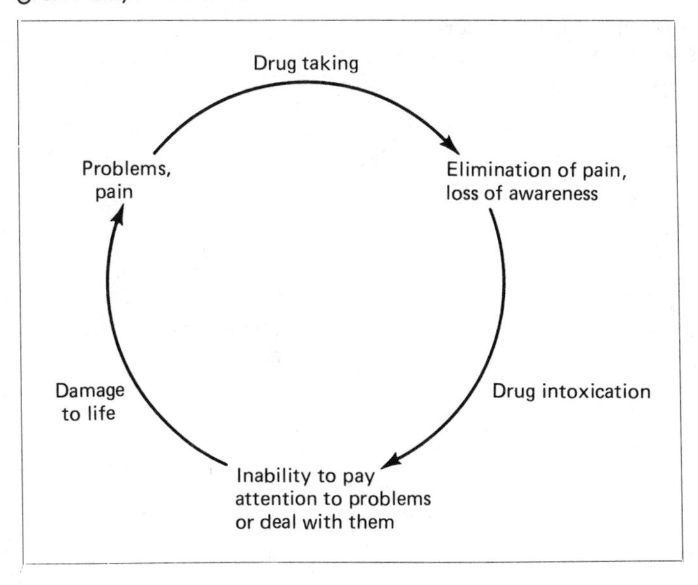

he will not enhance his capacity to understand what is going wrong with his family. He may, however, anger his wife and frighten his children when he comes home drunk.

While work and financial problems, and family and love problems, are usually part of an addiction, the greatest cause of pain—and hence of the desire to escape—lies within a person. If someone despises himself, the pain this feeling causes never leaves him. Thus the need for relief from that pain is constant. He can cover over the pain for a time through drug intoxication, but once he comes down from a drug high, or is no longer drunk, he feels even worse about himself. He has lost more respect from those whom he respects and feels guilty about the time and money he has spent to become unconscious. Thus the addiction cycle has an especially potent impact on a person's self-regard.

figure 1.2.
Addiction Cycle: Self-Regard.
A person's self-esteem is damaged through the addiction cycle.

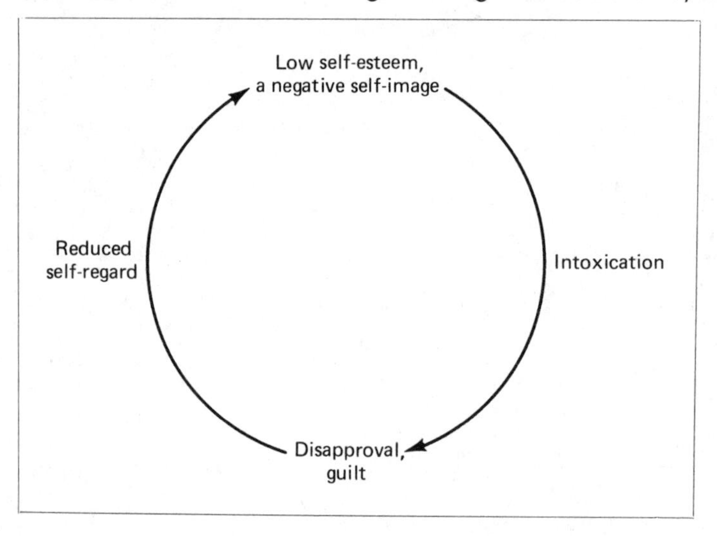

characteristics of an addictive experience

The addiction cycle makes clear the characteristics of an involvement with a drug which define that involvement as an addiction. These characteristics also tell us what kind of experience can be addictive. An addictive experience has the following hallmarks:

It eradicates awareness. To create the addiction cycle, a drug experience must eliminate a person's sense of pain by lessening his awareness of what is hurting or troubling him.

It hurts other involvements. The addiction cycle worsens when a drug experience makes a person less concerned about or less able to deal with other responsibilities. The person then turns increasingly toward the drug experience as his one source of gratification in life.

It lowers self-esteem. The chief casualty of an addictive experience is the addict's regard for himself.

It is not pleasurable. A popular misconception about drug addiction is that an addict takes a drug for pleasure. There is nothing pleasurable about the addiction cycle. All we need to do to assure ourselves of this is to think of a skid-row alcoholic. A person who lies unconscious on the street is not enjoying himself in any conventional sense of the word.

One reason for the misunderstanding surrounding the motives behind addiction is the confusion connected with defining pleasure. When the phrase "getting high" is applied to use of a depressant drug such as heroin or a barbiturate, it presents a misleading picture. A heroin user typically "nods

figure 1.3
The experience addicts seek from alcohol and other drugs is oblivion
From the WIZARD OF ID by permission of Johnny Hart and Field Enterprises, Inc.

out'' after shooting up; barbiturates encourage sleep. Both drugs—since they are analgesics—lessen or eliminate pain. In fact, then, what is ''pleasurable'' about addiction is the *absence* of feelings and thoughts that lead to pain. The experience is not one of *positive* pleasurable sensation.

It is predictable. Powerful depressant drugs are so effective as addictive objects not only because they lessen pain, but because they invariably produce the *same* effect. If a person drinks a fifth of vodka, for example, he knows what will happen to him. The addict who injects heroin into his bloodstream is fairly sure of how he will be feeling in a few minutes. It is this very *sureness* of effect the addicted person seeks.

To understand why this is so is to get at the heart of addiction. Addiction is a response to problems with which the individual feels he or she cannot cope. One of the addict's traits, however, is a diminished sense of self. Addicts lack confidence in their ability to cope generally, and as a result there are many things, including some of the challenges of a normal life, that they strive to avoid. Instead they prefer the safety of returning repeatedly to a predictable experience. An addiction exists when this need for constancy exceeds all other needs.

Withdrawal is not mentioned here as one of the characteristics of an addictive experience because it does not describe that experience. Rather, it is a separate but related experience which grows out of the person's involvement with an addictive experience. No drug has as a characteristic that it produces withdrawal; there are heavy users of all kinds of drugs who do not suffer withdrawal symptoms.

However, a person who is involved in a predictable experience that has ceased to bring him pleasure, but which he resorts to as a way of coping because it eradicates consciousness and pain, *will* undergo withdrawal. The reason comes from the addiction cycle, and from the destructive impact the addictive experience has on a person's other involvements. As he comes to rely on the experience to mask internal and external discomfort and stress, and as the experience becomes his sole source of gratification, the person cannot face a world in which the experience plays no part. To do so would mean confronting the hostile environment from which the drug experience has protected him. Afraid of doing so, missing the experience and the effects of the drug on his body, the person is now susceptible to withdrawal.

addictions to stimulants

We read earlier in this chapter about the addictive qualities of coffee (caffeine) and cigarettes (nicotine). Yet these drugs are stimulants and are totally distinct pharmacologically from the narcotics. How do stimulants fit into the addiction cycle so that they produce the addictive experience?

In the same way that people prefer different methods of dealing with thoughts or emotions, they can prefer different means of escaping from them. Research has shown habitual cigarette smokers to be more anxious than nonsmokers. However, when smoking, they report feeling less tense than usual, a relief that smoking does not bring people who are normally nonsmokers. Habitual smokers somehow find the stimulation of their nervous and circulatory systems—a stimulation that increases their heart rate, blood pressure, blood sugar, and general cardiac output—to be relaxing. Apparently, they become attuned to their excited internal state when smoking, and this inures them to external stimulation. Addicted smokers thus start to smoke when a potentially upsetting event occurs in order to ward off the anxiety this event would otherwise cause them.

As well as eradicating discomfort and pain, and a consciousness of one's problems, cigarette smoking fulfills other criteria of the addictive experience. By smoking, people limit their other opportunities in life; most noticeably by harming their health and perhaps shortening their lives. Especially now when there is such great consciousness of the harmfulness of cigarettes, people who continue to smoke court the disapproval of others, and by admitting that they cannot stop doing something that hurts them, decrease their own self-respect. Interestingly, research has shown that people whose self-esteem is higher find it easier to give up smoking.

Smoking also produces predictable sensations. It is in order to have these expected reactions that the smoker lights up. And, finally, although most smokers answer the question "Why do you smoke?" by saying that they enjoy it, smoking is no more pleasurable for a cigarette addict than drinking is for an alcoholic. People who smoke several packs a day lose the ability to savor the taste of tobacco—or practically anything else—after just a few smokes in the morning. The congestion and sore throat heavy smokers commonly report are sensations more omnipresent than the few pleasurable puffs they occasionally get from any cigarette after the first two or three. A popular antismoking program, in fact, asks smokers to describe just how pleasurable they expect their next smoke to be, ranking it from 1 to 10. The simple act of committing to paper the fact that they really don't look forward to enjoying a smoke is sobering for most smokers.

Caffeine addiction illuminates clearly the process of non-narcotic addiction. The coffee withdrawal symptoms we described earlier show up in people who cannot get by without a large intake of caffeine in the morning and throughout the day. For such people, normal means of obtaining energy—through exercise, diet, and rest—are not adequate. But at the same time that it energizes them, their caffeine high covers up the deficiencies that caused them to need a coffee pick-up in the first place. They become less aware of what it would take to supply this energy naturally, and more dependent on coffee to take up the slack. If they are, for example, bored at work, so that they droop at various points in the day, coffee rescues them in a way that does not help them to come to grips with the reason for their lethargy.

addictions that do not involve drugs

One woman reported to me that she stole candy bars from the grocery store when she didn't have enough money with her to buy them. She often ate until she made herself unconscious. As with any addiction, there are extreme cases. Yet the experience of this woman is familiar to other people with severe weight problems—and not totally foreign to many of the rest of us. Many people report that they feel relaxed only when they are surfeited with food, and that the act of eating relieves anxiety for them. They are searching for this relief when they shove food into their mouths long after they have ceased to note—or enjoy—the taste of the food itself. Certainly many people harm their ability to function through overeating.

Imagine a young person whose parents give him food as a reward when he behaves well or to quiet him when he whines or shows other signs of discontent. The child learns to comfort himself with food, and when life is difficult or unfulfilling, he has this predictable source of gratification to turn to. If he is fat, there will be few rewards for him at school, where the other children will make fun of him and where he will not be able to participate actively in sports. As he grows older, his efforts to achieve a normal social life may be so fruitless that he will refuse to take the risk. Instead he will return for gratification to the one activity—eating—whose immediate results he counts on, but whose long-range effects continue to make him miserable and to incapacitate him.

There are behavioral equivalents to the use of a stimulant

drug just as overeating parallels narcotic addiction. Recently, groups of Gamblers Anonymous have sprung up to deal with the growing number of people who spend a large portion of their lives at racetracks and casinos, or who fill their lives preparing bets and discussing the outcomes of their wagers with other gamblers. Some lyrically describe the mystique of gambling, the thrill of putting themselves in the hands of chance. The feeling is frightening and invigorating, taking their minds off everything else. The results, while seldom financially rewarding, are predictable. The heart leaps or the stomach sinks as victory or defeat materializes. Gamblers, moreover, seldom need to wait long to see how they have done—the outcome of a wager is usually apparent immediately. Some find even the wait of several minutes for a hand to be dealt or a race to be run too long. Thus a slot machine player stands transfixed in front of his machine, or two or three machines, feverishly feeding them and watching the figures appear, barely stooping to pick up his winnings should he hit the right combination.

For the person who finds escape in gambling, the world outside the casino or racetrack tends to become increasingly hostile. Family members who do not gamble are angered by the loss of significant portions of the family's income. The gambler's work suffers too, and should he decide that he needs more money to bet, and that he can steal it, even more damaging prospects await him. The typical story of a member of Gamblers Anonymous is that of a man whose wife and children have left him, who has lost a job and perhaps been charged with a crime, who—in short—has had his life destroyed by his habit.

interpersonal addictions

One other area of addiction seems unlikely at first, although it has long been recognized as such in song and in literature. This area is that explored in a book I wrote with Archie Brodsky, entitled *Love and Addiction.* Interpersonal relationships are among the most absorbing and reassuring of involvements. Especially in our culture—where "true love" is treasured and sought at the same time it seems to be becoming more and more difficult to obtain—the constant pursuit of a state of perfect love that forever proves illusory is at the center of many addictions.

There are a variety of addictive relationships, including that type in which couples are locked together in what they call love but what is actually a mutual enslavement or dependence. One indicator of the true nature of a relationship is whether or not those involved can deal with other people. When their tie to each other specifically prohibits other meaningful relationships of any kind, and jealousy is quickly aroused by others, addiction is probably present. The proof of the addiction is often found in what happens when the couple is separated. Since they are really using each other simply to fill a gap in their own lives, they may quickly turn to someone else for gratification. When this occurs, they are likely to turn against or forget entirely the previous lover, who is remembered not as a friend but as an enemy.

The motivations prompting such relationships are the same as those which cause other addictions. In all cases addicts are beset by insecurity and bad feelings about themselves. The addict in a relationship seeks to eradicate a painful self-consciousness either through the reassurance provided by the predictable presence of someone, or else through the excitement of constantly seeking the unattainable ideal lover. Both styles of addiction save him from the necessity of confronting himself and another person within the framework of a deepening relationship.

Realizing that a relationship as well as a drug can be addictive helps us to make sense of an otherwise puzzling phenomenon—the steadfastness with which some people hold on to a drug- or alcohol-addicted mate. The mate of the drug addict wants to be sure of his or her partner's "love," yet is too insecure to feel deserving of such dedication. The wife of an alcoholic, for example, may rely on her husband's drinking to give her a secure hold on her relationship with him. She knows he needs her, and also that it is unlikely anyone will compete with her for her position. The fact that her husband is an alcoholic not only guarantees that she is valued in the relationship, but gives her a sure means of controlling her mate. Since an inability to deal with the uncertainty and challenge of a normal existence is the main impetus for seeking the predictability of an addiction, the motives of the person addicted to a drug and those of his or her mate can be identical.

2
The sources of addiction

The addiction cycle centers around the person. It is with the individual that our analysis of the sources of addiction starts. At the same time, we cannot ignore the experiences people have had which predispose them to addiction. Their susceptibility to addiction is influenced by the groups they are part of, by society at large, and by the situations in which they find themselves. Ordinarily, it is those who doubt their capacity for realistic coping who seek experiences with addictive potential. What are the characteristics of such people?

internal sources of addiction

Fear of pain and failure. The key terms in our analysis of addiction in Chapter 1 were pain, anxiety, and fear. Certain people react less well to pain than others. They are more willing to demand a drug to help them deal with pain, and they are more likely to respond to even ordinary stimuli as painful.

When we talk about pain as a factor in addiction, we are not talking simply about the pain felt by hospital patients, although such pain is relevant. There is also a pain some people find in normal life—the pain of coping with everyday problems, of living with oneself, and of anticipating failure. Some people see all new or challenging events as carrying with them the vivid possibility of personal disaster. They have what is called a high fear of failure. Their behavior is characterized by efforts either to avoid risks altogether, or to take such great risks that failure is guaranteed and can therefore be excused. Fear of failure in children is sometimes noted experimentally when children are asked to toss a ring at a peg. Children who have high fear of failure are far more likely to stand close to the peg, so that it is almost impossible to miss, or to stand so far away that they have little chance of succeeding.

At the bottom of any addiction is fear, especially a person's fear of his own capacity to deal with his environment. This fear may be grounded in a correct sense the person has of his inadequacies, perhaps a recognition that he has not been equipped with sufficient education or training or that he has no opportunities to demonstrate what he can accomplish because of racial discrimination. However, feelings of inadequacy based on a realistic assessment of one's limitations often expand beyond their original basis in reality, and become a characteristic way of responding to the world that makes it impossible for a person to see opportunities where they exist, or to accept success when it is within reach.

Addiction is certainly not limited to oppressed minorities. Nor is it solely the province of the disabled or incompetent. This is because fear of failure may be unrelated to a person's actual ability. And the experience of success does not always eliminate these feelings. There are many people who command the respect of others because of their actions but are consumed with self-doubt. When successful people who become addicted to drugs or alcohol are questioned, they often say that they always feared being uncovered as frauds. The strain produced by the discrepancy between their outward performance and their feelings of inadequacy drove them to seek unconsciousness through alcohol or other drugs.

A negative self-image. People with low self-esteem lack confidence in themselves or their abilities. In some cases, this negative self-image develops into self-hate. A person despises himself so greatly that he tries to harm himself, perhaps not obviously, but through behavior that damages his health or otherwise detracts from his life. In becoming a drug addict, a person may be acting out the image he has of himself, taking the negative role society assigns to him as being that which he deserves.

Dependency, passivity, and an external orientation. Addiction entails reliance on an outside mechanism in order to cope. Addicts are always looking for external solutions to life's problems. Thus they are more likely to think, for example, that having a certain job or a certain possession would make their lives better. Often they have been brought up to depend excessively on other people, for example they may have had clinging relationships with members of their family. Their lack of self-confidence often causes them to seek out people on whom they can rely to get them what they need.

Looking to others or to external forces to solve problems is the opposite of an active orientation toward life. People who have such an attitude tend to wait for things to happen rather than pursuing them, to accept whatever is offered or reject it without seeking alternatives, and to be unable to move from complaints or resentment to constructive action. Frequently, they feel that they cannot take charge of their lives; that even to try to do so would be futile. They find addicition is an easier response to problems than attempting to solve them.

Values and beliefs. Since addictions are by definition unhealthy, people who are addicted are harming themselves in some way, often physically. People vary widely in their concern for their own well-being. Some learn from an early age to eschew anything that might limit them, and no matter what other personality traits they have they refuse to smoke or drink. Other people are careless about their diet or their use of drugs, and they readily do things that damage their health.

Although abstinence from alcohol or cigarettes tends to run in families, prohibitions against such things as smoking and drinking must be internalized in order to be effective. Thus Mormons and members of religious sects that discourage the use of alcohol–when they do drink–end up drinking excessively far more frequently than the average person. This is because they have not really learned to be moderate and health-seeking in their habits. They have learned simply to avoid drinking, and once this rule is broken there is nothing to guide their behavior along positive lines.

One learned characteristic that is crucial in determining people's susceptibility to addiction is their readiness to believe in magical solutions to problems. A magical solution is one which cannot affect the actual situation, but which reassures the person nonetheless. Examples of magical solutions are prayer, fantasy, superstition, and mind-altered states. Not everyone who prays for a miracle or fantasizes about a problem going away is an addict, of course. Some situations are irremediable, and seeking spiritual solace becomes the most human thing to do. Also, such behavior may be constructive when it galvanizes a person to act along constructive lines. For example, praying or meditating may give a person the strength actually to deal with a troublesome matter. Even becoming intoxicated occasionally may make some people able to relax so that they can better meet their professional and personal obligations.

On the other hand, the illusion some people have that because a problem is out of mind, it has gone away, can convince them that they need to take no further action in reality. They lose what motivation they had to resolve their problems. Thus people who meditate, smoke, or take tranquilizers may persuade themselves that they have less to be anxious about, while this may not be true in the least. This variety of escapism is one that is also learned within the family. Its opposite is the development of the ability to identify one's feelings and their sources outside of oneself, and to act on this awareness so as to make a difference in one's life.

external sources of addiction

Most people's susceptibility to addiction is not constant. It varies with the stages of their lives and the settings in which they find themselves. It is correct to say that much addiction is socially caused—for example, by ghetto conditions that make people hopeless about their future. Identifying situations that increase the likelihood of addiction helps us to understand the conditions of addiction.

Life stages. There are common crises in human life—crises everyone experiences to some degree—that upset people to the point where addictive experiences become more inviting. One period of particular vulnerability is adolescence. It is in this period that most people who become addicts develop the habits that dog them as adults. Cigarette smoking, drinking to excess, heroin usage, and other forms of drug abuse nearly always begin in adolescence, as youngsters emerging into adulthood face pressures with which they are not yet prepared to cope. Addictions are based primarily on the fear of being unable to cope with life. Nearly all adolescents have some self-doubt on this score, and those whose parents have been especially overprotective or whose upbringing has incapacitated them in some other way frequently learn at this time to rely on chemical aids to maintain their psychological equilibrium.

The other side of the coin is that the excesses adolescence produces are often not permanent. As people grow to fill the roles that are expected of them, and as they gain acceptance from others and the confidence to proceed with life, these early addictions may be left behind. Among those who deal with heroin addicts, this phenomenon is referred to as "maturing out." Because the process of developing addictions in adolescence and outgrowing them in adulthood is so common, it might almost be termed normal for a person to be addicted to something at some point in life.

What *is* a troubling sign is when a person is unable to find greater maturity with age. For example, an older film star who married a very young woman announced that she was the "real love" of his life, only to kick her out of his house several weeks later. He was showing a type of immaturity that is seriously disabling to a human being. While it is not surprising for a teenager to mistake sexual infatuation for "love," in an adult the inability to discriminate between these emotions is psychopathological.

Periods of pain. One of the persistent anomalies in the field of addiction research has been the fact that hospital patients who are given narcotics rarely become addicted to them. In fact, most of these people don't even notice any withdrawal symptoms when they leave the hospital, although they have been taking narcotics for several weeks in doses far stronger than those available to the average street addict. This is because withdrawal does not come from a drug, but from the nature of a person's involvement with an experience. People who do not require a narcotic experience as a regular concomitant to their existence do not suffer withdrawal when a drug is discontinued. The need for the pain-eliminating effects of a drug will vary with the presence or absence of pain. If the pain people feel is temporary, their need for a narcotic will not last. On the other hand, periods of extreme pain can drive people—even those not ordinarily predisposed in that direction—to become addicted for a time. Whether a person breaks out of the addiction cycle or simply exchanges one addiction for another—as is the case, for instance, when a person stops smoking only to begin overeating—depends on whether the person has dealt with the issues underlying his or her addiction. This can be relatively easy for a hospital patient whose pain disappears as do post-operative stitches. In other situations, quite a bit more effort will be required to root out the sources of addiction.

One stressful situation that only some experience (unlike adolescence) is war. The Vietnam war was the scene of the largest experiment in drug use in our history. Upwards of a third of the American soldiers in Vietnam tried a narcotic at least once, and most of those who used heroin or opium did so repeatedly over an extended period. It was, therefore, with great trepidation that American authorities viewed the home-coming of these men. What actually happened went against all existing notions of drug addiction: most of the soldiers gave up their drug habits without any difficulty once they left Vietnam. A follow-up study was conducted of soldiers who had shown a positive trace of a narcotic in their urine when they were tested by the military. Of these "drug positive" soldiers, fully three-quarters reported that they had indeed been addicted in Vietnam. However, only seven percent showed signs of dependence at home, *even though one-third continued to use a narcotic at least occasionally.* As the researchers put it, "contrary to conventional belief, the occasional use of narcotics without becoming addicted appears possible even for men who have previously been dependent on narcotics."

This phenomenon is not really surprising when we consider the characteristics that cause addiction. The elements in the Vietnam setting that led soldiers to be addicted are the same as those encountered elsewhere by people who become addicts. However, the feelings they experienced temporarily because of the war are a permanent part of the make-up and outlook of the ordinary addict.

Altogether, the Vietnam experience makes clear what kind of pressures will drive a person otherwise not addiction-prone to become an addict. For many soldiers in combat areas, fear and discomfort were everpresent. Not only were these men in danger of losing their lives, but they were deprived of the security and reassurance people expect from their environments. Not all the soldiers who were addicted to heroin in Vietnam were in combat situations and hence in active danger. However, they *were* all out of control of their lives—that is, their basic life choices were not in their own hands. As we have seen, a feeling of powerlessness—of being unable to influence one's situation in a positive way—is as great a factor in addiction as fear.

Also of crucial importance for the soldier addict was the absence of close relationships and the loss of meaningful work. Without their families, lovers, wives, and life-long friends to provide intimacy, they looked to narcotics for substitute gratification. At the same time, the narcotic experience covered over the futility of their individual actions as well as the futility of the overall war effort. Without the gratification that comes from rewarding work or from intimate human relationships, the allure of the narcotic experience in Vietnam was overwhelming for these men.

the influence of groups, culture, and society

It is commonplace to note the influence of the group on the individual in all areas of behavior, drug-taking among them. People tend to travel in units of like-minded individuals, so that a boy or girl who associates with a crowd of heavy drinkers will naturally tend to drink a lot. A group may also introduce, or socialize, an individual into a pattern of drug-taking. Research has shown that not only does a person usually learn to take a drug from friends and members of his social group, but he also learns from others how to react to a drug. In Vietnam, heroin users in a given unit would show the same kinds of withdrawal symptoms, which might be very different from those felt by soldiers in other units. The power of the group is such that in a setting like the treatment center Daytop Village, where the group disapproves of withdrawal, an addict frequently suppresses his symptoms entirely.

One of the most important determinants of whether a person will control his use of a given substance or become addicted to it is the models for moderate use he has around him. We have seen that alcoholics are more likely to come from families where drinking was either excessive or totally prohibited. Studies of people who use narcotics in a controlled way find that such users know other people who limit their drug use so that they can cope with jobs or schoolwork. It is the absence of examples of moderate patterns of usage that makes it difficult for individuals to arrive at such patterns themselves.

Often, the group from which an individual learns how to take—and react to—a substance is a cultural group. For example, different cultures have different attitudes toward alcohol. They feel differently not only about how much drinking should be done and when it is proper to imbibe, but about the very meaning of drinking. Among some groups, such as the Irish or Native Americans, there is a very high percentage of problem drinkers. Among other groups, such as the Greeks and Italians, problem drinking is practically unknown.

To understand why these differences exist, we have to return to the history and significance of alcohol in a culture. Native Americans were introduced to the drinking of alcohol by white men, and alcohol came to symbolize the subjugation of their race. There are quite a few examples of this process in history, most recently among the Inupiat of Alaska's North Slope. The abuse of opium by the Chinese was associated with western domination of China in the nineteenth century. Tobacco was used as an intoxicant—it was smoked to the point of unconsciousness—by the Hottentots and other native peoples of South Africa when it was brought to that part of the world by Europeans (who had in turn borrowed it from the natives of the new world and subsequently abused it). On the other hand, opium and heroin are normally not objects of addiction and extreme public reaction in the Asian cultures from which Americans obtain their narcotic supplies.

The Irish tradition of drinking derives from that of the Gaelic culture which has inspired many modern Irish customs and styles. Almost perpetually at war, Celtic men would gather the night before a battle in their leader's tent to drink until dawn. It was considered normal for several fights in which men were killed to break out during these drinking sessions. The Mediterranean style of drinking is entirely different. First, a child learns to drink at home, where alcohol is taken with family meals and its use is regulated by social custom. When Italian or Greek men gather to drink, alcohol is consumed in a social setting accompanied by good-natured conversation and convivial interaction. Alcohol is a social lubricant, and is not seen as an excuse for antisocial or aggressive behavior.

Once in North Beach, an Italian area of San Francisco, I

was with a group of Italian Americans who were having their weekly Saturday get-together. One of the men had brought a friend, a WASP from one of the Southern states. As the afternoon progressed and each person bought a round of drinks in turn, this guest became more and more unruly, harrassing the waitress and losing his composure generally. The regular drinkers became more and more disapproving, and finally the man who had brought the outsider along was forced to take him home. As he left with his friend, he told the by now drunken social offender, "That isn't how we do it here."

Researchers have shown that the fantasies associated with drinking vary from culture to culture, and from individual to individual. In a culture where there is a preoccupation with power, often because many people are deprived of it, drinking engenders feelings of omnipotence, and drunkenness often leads to fights, crime, reckless driving, or other antisocial behavior. It is these cultures that have high rates of alcoholism. Where the act of drinking does not have these connotations, alcoholism may be practically nonexistent.

When we remember that it is an *experience* rather than a substance to which a person becomes addicted, we can see that drinking is only capable of producing an addiction for people in certain circumstances. If a man doubts his potency, drinking may allow him to believe that he is powerful and respected. When intoxicated he may try to dominate other people in line with this alcohol-inspired self-image. The behavior he engages in, however, incurs disapproval and social sanctions. Thus when he ceases to be intoxicated, his disgust with himself as well as his objective situation will have worsened, and alcohol may be his only refuge once again.

Of course, alcoholism is only one form of addiction, and different cultural backgrounds predispose people to have different areas of weakness. For example, whereas Italian Americans and Jewish Americans have low rates of alcoholism, they are more likely to be overweight. These groups often give food an emotional meaning it doesn't have for other groups, and eating comes to produce an experience that is reinforcing but debilitating in a way that encourages the addiction cycle. Other group experiences are so destructive that they promote a host of addictions. Black Americans, because they frequently face destructive physical and social environments, more often fall prey to addictions to alcohol, smoking, illicit drugs, gambling, and food.

Stresses that cause large groups of people to be addiction-prone are not limited to blacks. According to the head of the National Institute on Drug Abuse, alcohol and drug abuse among young Americans is epidemic. What might cause a whole society to move in this direction? The typical addict feels that he has little control over what happens to him in life. If many people in a culture feel this way, rates of addiction will increase culturewide. The young person in America today faces an overwhelmingly complex society, and one in which opportunities for achievement are daily more limited. This alone should not cause a jump in addiction. In addition, however, people no longer seem to have confidence in their ability to handle deviations from familiar patterns. Somehow our basic institutions—family, school, work, and love relationships—are not giving us the security and sense of competence we need to proceed in a world that has become less orderly.

3

Complexities in evaluating addiction:

Disease notions and partial addictions

Reading the previous chapters, one might decide that everything is addictive. This is true to the extent that any compelling experience *can be* an addiction. But no activity is in and of itself addictive; it simply depends on the way a person chooses to engage in the activity. And, finally, not all the indicators of addiction may point in the same direction. Some addictive criteria may be fulfilled while others are not. The greatest error made in thinking about addiction is to see it as an all-or-nothing phenomenon. Addiction is one end of a continuum of behavior. Somewhere along that continuum are to be found habits, then dependencies and compulsions. Addiction is an extreme along this dimension—it is a pathological habit or dependency.

The previous chapters may also have convinced readers that addicts are completely crippled, characterized as they are by so many debilitating personality traits. Again the truth is more complex. A person need not have all characteristics of the addicts I have described in order to be addicted. Moreover there are people who have many of these traits who avoid

figure 3.1.
Addiction Is One End of a Continuum.
Habits may be arranged in terms of a dimension of addictiveness.

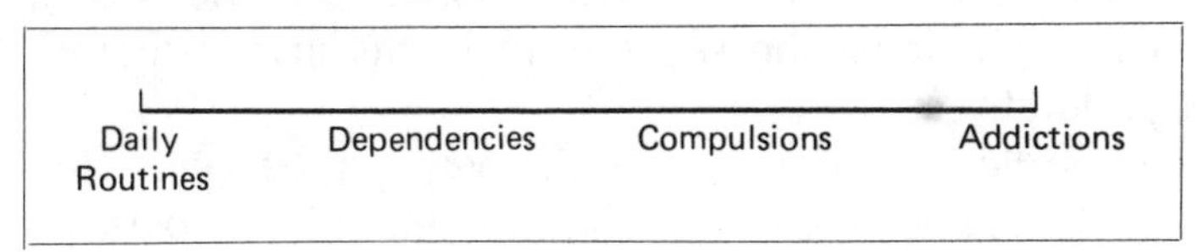

addiction. Usually this is because they have overriding strengths or values that prevent them from yielding to addiction. Overall, addicts are not so different from the rest of the population; we all have elements of "the addictive personality" within us awaiting the proper set of circumstances to appear. What is more, we have all had addictive experiences in our lives, even if we have not allowed an addiction to dominate our existence.

Because addiction, like all behavior, is so complex and involves so many variables, we cannot always state positively that an addiction does or does not exist. We can use the criteria for addiction—as well as utilizing other signs of addiction or nonaddiction—to help us make a qualitative assessment, but more often than not, we will be unable to arrive at a definitive answer. In fact, wanting finally and absolutely to label an involvement as either a positive habit or an addiction is a mark of a compulsiveness akin to addiction.

signs of addiction

An addiction exists when a person ceases to be able to make choices. If, in contemplating whether to do something, a person is no longer able to consider whether it is the proper time for the activity, if he isn't sensitive to his own moods in considering the activity, and if nothing else can seriously compete with the activity for his interest, he is in danger of being addicted. The mark of addiction here is *inflexibility.* It appears also in a person's approach to an activity. When a person no longer varies the amount of time he devotes to something, the way he does it, or the challenge he seeks from it, his involvement is becoming addictive.

As an addictive involvement deepens, it becomes less enjoyable. This does not lessen the strength of the person's attachment to the involvement, because the addict's goal is not pleasure but constancy. He is seeking primarily to have the same experience every time. We know this not only because he does not want—in fact he eschews—variation, but because he engages in the activity more as a way of avoiding other things than because of its intrinsic value. Chief among the things he is avoiding is his sense of inadequacy. A man who unthinkingly turns on the television the moment he has an opportunity to do so does not particularly care what is playing. He doesn't turn a show off because it is boring or inconsequential. Nor does he think about what other things he could do with his time, for example, talk with his wife or children. Actually, the more his family's health requires that he pay attention to them, the more he may be driven to the TV as an alternative to dealing with this real need. The anxiety he already feels about his life increases, and hence he welcomes even more the unconsciousness his addiction offers.

An addictive activity that enables a person to forget his problems may continue until the matters he is ignoring become so alarming that he must do something about them. Even then, a person in the final stages of addiction may not be capable of responding to real pressures. The keynote of addiction is that it destroys a person's ability to cope with or gain gratification from anything else. As we have noted, one of the chief casualties of addiction is self-esteem. While this is evident in the case of drug addictions, it may be less clear when an addictive activity is socially approved or offers some benefits. Yet the same esteem-destroying criterion appears in such activities as well. Although a person may come to feel better about his capacity in one area, in an addiction the beneficial impact of an activity does not carry over to other aspects of the person's life. Hence rather than enhancing the person's overall self-esteem, the activity becomes a refuge to which he can turn to hide his insecurities.

disease theories of addiction

A woman appearing on a talk show was describing her alcoholism. She said, "You know that you're an alcoholic when drinking harms your life; it's that simple. For me, becoming an alcoholic was a gradual process. I think that you'll rarely find that a person has one drink and goes over the edge. I just found it harder and harder to cope. Coping was something I was always weak at, which was a good part of the problem in the first place." When the interviewer asked the woman who was responsible for her condition, she answered, "No one is responsible. What I didn't know that I have since found out is that alcoholism is a disease like diabetes—you are born with an allergy to alcohol." This last idea is one that has been promoted by Alcoholics Anonymous and related groups, and has been picked up by the medical establishment. Today it is the dominant concept in the field of alcoholism and addiction generally. Groups like Gamblers Anonymous take the same position, claiming that compulsive gambling is likewise a disease.

Addiction is not in any sense a disease. In fact, one strong piece of evidence that it is not is that activities like gambling, which involve no abuse of a substance and therefore no physical predilection toward addiction, create the same syndrome as other addictions. There are good reasons why the woman in the interview accepts the idea that alcoholism is a disease. For one thing, it very usefully permits her and others to avoid the guilt drinking causes, which is one of the continuing sources of addiction. However, everything she actually says about herself and her feelings goes against the notion that alcoholism is a disease. For example, she mentions that one important cause of her drinking was the difficulties she *always* had in coping. Why should someone with an allergy to alcohol independently have this problem? Is it by some mysterious coincidence that the "disease" of alcoholism and ineffectiveness in dealing with the world are both found in the same person?

Furthermore, this woman describes her—and most people's—descent into alcoholism as a gradual process. Yet the disease theory presupposes that some people have a distinct proclivity in their bodily make-up that causes them to overreact to the drug. Recently, Al Hodge, TV's Captain Video, died alone and broke in a rundown Manhattan hotel. His wife reported leaving him because of his accelerating alcoholism, a problem that had surfaced when he was unable to find work. Time and again we see Hollywood notables and others who suddenly discover that they are alcoholics when their careers disintegrate. What is clearly true here—that some people slip into a state of alcoholism during trying periods in their lives, and that they may stay there when there is no prospect of reviving their careers—tells us much about alcoholism, but nothing about a person's inbred and unalterable susceptibility to alcohol.

The reason I am at such pains to refute the notion that alcoholism is a disease is that such a theory is not helpful to many people—including those whose drinking does not reach the stage of constant intoxication, and those who are not comfortable in the totalitarian atmosphere of Alcoholics Anonymous. What, for example, would we say about a woman who drinks at social gatherings in order to overcome her insecurities? By seeking a physical cause for her "alcoholism," we ignore the real cause of her drinking—a lack of confidence about dealing with other people. Because she doesn't drink to the point of unconsciousness we might refuse to label her an alcoholic. On the other hand, not recognizing the cause of her drinking could readily allow it to grow to more dangerous proportions as the woman fails to come to grips with her sense of inadequacy.

A host of studies have established what is also commonsensical: that there are different types of drinking problems—just as there are different varieties of any social and psychological problem. Some of these studies were attacked almost before they were published. For example, the initial Rand Report on alcoholism agreed with every systematic study on alcoholism conducted before it when it found that there are a number of long-range solutions to alcoholism, including total abstinence *and* a return to moderate drinking. Press conferences were convened simultaneously around the country *on the day the report was released* to attack its findings and to label them as dangerous. Today, addiction has become a topic that cannot be discussed rationally. And those millions of people—including the growing number of adolescents—who have a drinking problem but who cannot identify with the disease model and the AA treatment are given no clues to the reasons for their condition.

"partial" addictions

Another complexity in evaluating addictions is the seemingly partially addicted individual. If addiction is part of a person's physical or psychological make-up, how can it be limited to one area of his life? The disease theory of addiction offers no explanation for this phenomenon since there is no way to account for a disease that regularly disappears when a person is in certain circumstances. On the other hand, one of the hallmarks of addiction as defined by the addiction cycle is that it tends to grow until there is no room in a person's life for other, healthy pursuits. Can there be, then, some cases in which an addiction is not all consuming?

The part-time alcoholic. A man came to me for advice about his daughter. She was nineteen, had a child, was separated from her husband, and had recently been hospitalized because of her reliance on drugs. Since I wasn't speaking with the daughter, I began by exploring her father's relationship with her. In the course of my discussions with him I discovered that he was a partner in a small but profitable machine shop, that he lived alone with his wife of over twenty years, and that he drank himself into a stupor every evening after dinner and all weekend. Each morning that he awoke with the prospect of going to work in mind, however, he felt happy and refreshed. He never drank on the job. The man acknowledged no connection between his behavior and his daughter's problems.

This individual had a tremendously long way to go to recognize the patterns in his own life and the patterns his daughter was following. One might say that he had spent the last twenty years—or longer—avoiding having to think about these things. His drinking had been going on practically as long as his marriage, yet he had never taken it as indicating a need for change. Whereas he felt comfortable and confident about his job skills and the business he had helped to found, he was at a loss in intimate family relationships. It is hard to assess a person like this in terms of the usual addictive criteria and the personal qualities that tend to underlie addiction. He was not fearful at work, and while working he did not avoid challenges or seek only predictable outcomes. Hence he was actually not an addict at work, though he was one at home.

The workaholic. One of the most popular addictive designations is that of *workaholic.* Many people find this term both accurate and appealing, yet they do not always take the label seriously. Can working constitute a genuine addiction?

The chairman of the board of directors of one large American company had six children. None of them got through college without first dropping out and undergoing some emotional turmoil. When the last of his children had graduated from high school, almost as though this man were relieved of an obligation, he divorced his wife and married his secretary. I spoke with one of the man's sons about his relationship with his father. Once, after school, the son had been picked up by the police for participating in a prank with some other teenagers. The father was called from work to the police station to pick up the boy. He was furious, a state his son had never seen him in before. Later the boy surmised that it was because he had broken the peaceful mold of the family routine, and forced his father to notice that there was a problem at home, that had upset the man so greatly.

Several years later, when the boy was in college, he was able to wangle an invitation to accompany a friend's father to view a presentation his own father was making to the business community. His father was surprised and reserved when he saw his son, again as though he felt demands were being made of him that were alien to his way of life. The man typically worked fifteen hours a day, rarely seeing his children except on weekends. He always appeared awkward to his children when he was called on to discipline them or speak to them. Yet he was supremely successful, and confident, in the business world. His son said that seeing his father speak to a gathering of important business people and public figures gave him an impression he had never before gotten of his father. The son had needed to attend the meeting in order to be able to understand how the stiff and unsure person he knew at home was at the same time a prominent and capable person.

When a discrepancy this large exists in a person's ability to handle different parts of his life, there is a natural tendency for the person to prefer one part to the other. If a preference for a work environment is reinforced by others and approved by society at large because of the success it brings, other aspects of life can easily be shunted aside. A person may seek all his gratifications from work, justifying his absorption with his job by saying that he is working to provide for his family. But when he has a choice between being with his family and working, he will always choose work. To do otherwise would be to thrust himself into an uncertain situation and to deprive himself of the reassurance and rewards he depends on.

Is this person an addict? Certainly withdrawal can occur when a person stops working. One man, taking his first vacation in years, found that he couldn't get to sleep in his Florida condominium. Instead, he flew home in the middle of the night so that he could get to work the next day. Work can produce withdrawal because it is absorbing, allowing a person to forget problems in other areas of life; because, for someone who is successful, it is a reliable source of gratification; and because it may be done compulsively rather than because it is genuinely satisfying. An overemphasis on work will also harm nonwork involvements, as when it destroys a marriage and lessens the time available for other activities. But it does not seem to fulfill the criterion that an addiction must detract from one's self-esteem. Most people who work every possible moment are proud of what they do and are acknowledged for the contributions they make. Yet it is only in the work setting that they can feel good about themselves, and so the identity work supports is very limited and easily upset.

figure 3.2.
A "Partial" Addiction Cycle.
A simultaneous positive and negative cycle can exist in a person's life. If on balance the person's functioning is impaired, an addiction can be said to exist.

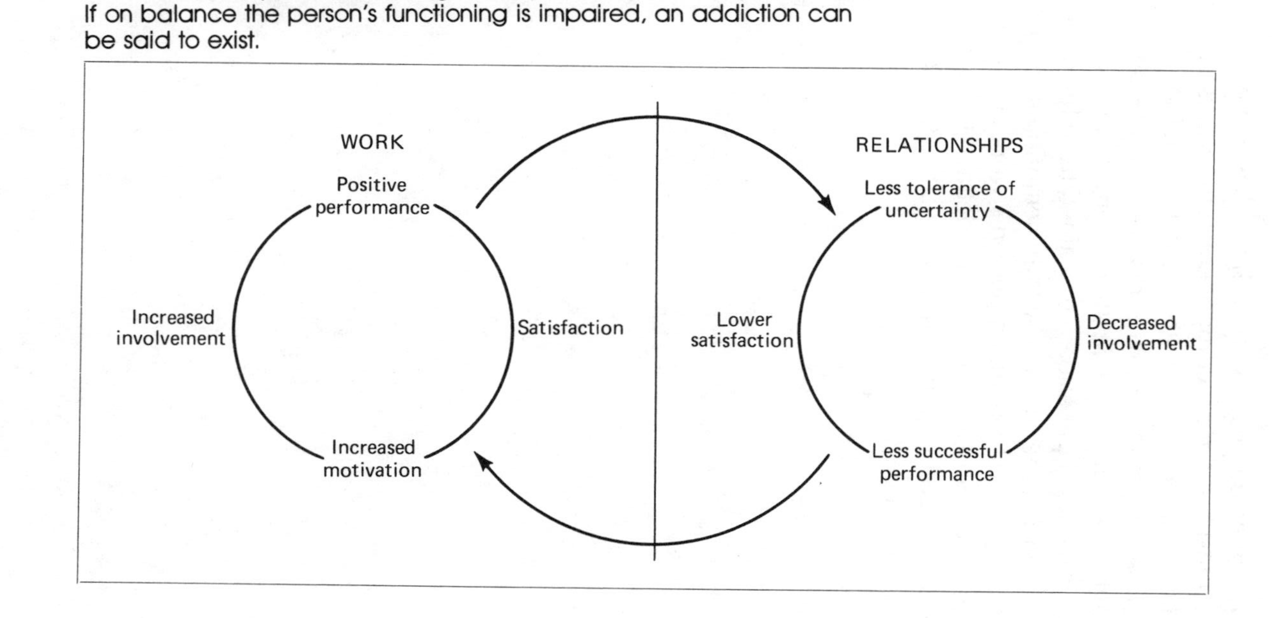

To judge whether someone is being harmed by an involvement, we must look at all components of the person's life. The man addicted to work in our story failed as a father and created unhappiness for his family. Yet this was not the only path he could have taken given his relative strengths and weaknesses. He might have used the esteem he gained from his professional life to help him come to grips with his emotional limitations. It makes sense, then, to say that a person's work activities, if they fail to help him outside work, can detract from his overall confidence and competence. In this way, the final criterion for addiction is satisfied.

4

Distinguishing addictions from healthy habits:

Running

The definition of—and criteria for—addiction do not allow a habit to be simultaneously healthy *and* addictive. An addiction is something that, on balance, hurts an individual's functioning. The fact that an involvement originally has a healthy impact, or at least is intended to have one, does not change its nature as an addiction should it fulfill all the addictive criteria. Not only does such a habit have all the significant characteristics of an addiction, but its genesis in the individual's life is the same as that of any other addiction.

It is necessary to apply the criteria for addiction to overcome the confusion that stems from the "healthy" label an activity has. For nothing is invariably healthy just as nothing is invariably addictive: it is the nature of the person's relationship to the activity that causes it to be one thing or the other. If someone drinks alcohol in moderate amounts to celebrate important events, and if doing so brings good feelings and enhances the companionship of others, then drinking can be a healthy habit. On the other hand, if an activity produces positive results for a person—as working may—but grows to overshadow everything else in the person's life, its positive impact will be submerged by its negative consequences.

Perhaps no healthful activity within memory has achieved the place in American consciousness that running has. It is now difficult for a health-conscious individual to *avoid* exposure to running, and certainly great numbers of Americans do jog or run. But along with the overwhelming popularity of this activity has come a backlash. There are, for example, articles and books that provide nonrunners with ammunition against those who constantly proselytize for running. Many nonrunners have tried running and found that it didn't fit their lifestyle. Yet they find it hard not to be defensive about the fact that they don't run.

Nonrunners' guides or revelations are often written with tongue in cheek; more serious have been a number of articles pointing up the dangers connected with excessive running. These dangers include the slighting of one's family and one's work to run, running to a point where bodily damage results and then continuing to run, and psychological dislocations that occur when heavy runners are forced to stop running. Although it is silly to blame these negative outcomes on running *per se*, what makes the growing realization that running can be hazardous interesting is the fact that this form of exercise has been welcomed so wholeheartedly in health circles for its beneficial effects. It has been proposed as an all-purpose solution for a host of physical and psychological ills. But as the following story shows, whatever drives people to continue doing something to the point where it becomes harmful is as likely to be present in runners as it is in other human beings.

a runner's tale

Jim was active athletically in high school and college, but when he attended graduate school in biology his rate of exercise slowed down considerably. This trend continued after graduation when he took a job in a big city medical center and got married. He went from his apartment to work and back daily without ever breaking into a sweat. Three years after he started his job he had gained over thirty pounds, he was smoking over a pack of cigarettes a day, and many of his social evenings were spent drinking with friends.

Jim tended to overdo things in many ways. Some people, for example, found his behavior toward his wife to be egregious. He demanded that she do all the household chores even though she also worked, he dominated her socially by monopolizing the conversation when they were together, and he expected her to anticipate all his needs. Jim was surprised when his wife asked for a divorce (though his friends and acquaintances were not). In fact, he was crushed. Besides not knowing what to do without his wife, he was alarmed at the prospect of having to find other women to date. In truth, he was embarrassed by his obesity and by his general lack of physical conditioning.

While Jim occasionally played softball or touch football on weekends, he knew that these activities could not provide him with enough exercise to get in shape. Taking his cue from several cardiologists who also worked at the medical center, Jim began jogging. The first time out he could not go a quarter of a mile without stopping. By the end of the week he could do a half-mile; in a month he was able to run a mile. He continued running regularly for nearly two years, gradually increasing his distance from one mile to three. He also stopped smoking and changed his eating habits. He looked and felt good.

As Jim went on his daily jog, more serious runners would spurt past him on their workouts. This never bothered Jim, for he thought of these men as different from himself. He was in awe of them. After several years of running, however, he began considering what he might do to enliven his workouts. He had a new girlfriend, and she mentioned to him that someone she knew was entered in a five-mile race to be held several months in the future. Jim became taken with the idea of running the race. To prepare for it he forced himself to run five miles a day. He stuck to this schedule religiously until the race, which he ran in a modest time that enabled him to finish approximately in the middle of the pack.

Jim was exultant. Until the race, he had never considered himself a real runner. After it, he began training with fresh energy. If the truth were known, Jim did not particularly like his work. He was essentially an exalted technician who had long ago realized that he didn't have the drive or ability to be an original researcher. As for his social life, he had been seeing his woman friend for about six months. They enjoyed spending weekends and several nights a week together. In addition, Jim called the woman on the evenings they didn't meet to talk for an hour or so. They were now planning on being married.

Within this framework, Jim resolved to up his mileage. After all, making the jump to five miles a day hadn't been too difficult. Whereas once he would never have believed he could go beyond three miles, it was now *only* at the three-mile point in his run that he became invigorated and relaxed. In order to extend the period of good feeling, he increased his regular run first to seven and then to eight miles. At this point Jim—who had been running during his lunch break at work—realized that he would have to change his schedule. Counting getting to a place where he could run, a limbering-up period, and the time he spent taking a shower, his daily running ritual now consumed close to three hours. He began to run at night after work.

The shift to nighttime running naturally cut into other activities, particularly those involving his fiancee, Diane. Jim could rarely eat before nine o'clock, and he could no longer participate in more involved social encounters during the week. Whereas previously he and Diane had tried to attend at least one event such as a ballet or a movie on a week night, Jim's running now ruled this out. Diane was able to tolerate this, however, since she often worked late at her job at an advertising agency. What was more of a problem was the contentiousness that had entered their relationship with Jim's running. Jim had induced Diane to run for a time, but she had dropped out. Jim couldn't believe that Diane didn't enjoy running the way he did, and so he continued to press her to take it up again. When Diane suggested that she might prefer aerobic dancing as an alternative method of getting exercise, Jim cut her off with an abrupt, "Dancing is no good." Jim himself no longer participated in other sports he had enjoyed, such as softball or football, for fear of incurring a muscle strain that would hinder his running.

In truth, reading, talking and day-dreaming about running took up the better part of Jim's time when he was not actually running. He brought all his conversations around to running at some point, and forever encouraged friends either to jog or—if they already jogged—to enter a race. Jim counted it as a triumph when he got a new person involved in running. Once they had taken this step, he would try to describe to them the joy—the "runner's high"—that came from running longer distances. Yet one of Jim's major disappointments was the absence of regular running companions. He found it difficult to modify the length or the speed of his workouts to accommodate other runners, and sooner or later all the people he had introduced to running bowed out of jogging with him.

Running the mileage he did after his first race, Jim was training as hard as the "professional" runners he saw when he worked out. He realized that he was now on a regimen that would allow him to run a marathon with them. The word "marathon" had always produced for Jim extravagant fantasies; it seemed to him to belong to another world. Without immediately announcing that he was planning to enter a marathon, he did begin to train for one. He now ran ten miles a day, and did one twenty-mile run each weekend for two months before the marathon he planned to enter.

Around this time Jim met a young doctor at work who was also preparing for the marathon and whose schedule corresponded somewhat to Jim's. Although this man didn't devote the same amount of time to running that Jim did, he and Jim generally ran together at least twice a week for company and to exchange runner's hints and stories. The prospect of a 26-mile run still intimidated Jim, and he spoke about being lucky to be able to finish. It was for this reason that he ran twenty miles on weekends. His friend eschewed these runs, pointing out that experienced runners considered it overtraining to do more than one or two twenty-mile runs in preparation for a marathon.

For some reason, his doctor friend was not as anxious about the big race as Jim. This man seemed to feel that he would be able to summon the necessary reserves of energy when the time came. Jim, for his part, was petrified by the fabled "wall" marathoners reported running into sometime after the twenty-mile mark. Perhaps it was because of this that Jim found running with his friend reassuring. On marathon day they ran together for nearly the entire course, despite the fact that both acknowledged Jim's superior conditioning. In the last mile, still feeling strong, Jim went ahead of his companion. He finished feeling strong.

For several weeks Jim basked in the glory of his completed marathon; he had known nothing that compared with it. Then he started running strenuously again. His plans were upset, however, when his friend indicated that he didn't want to continue running as seriously as before, that he was dropping back to five-mile runs a few times a week. Jim, for his part, hoped to continue doing eight miles a day for the entire year, and to intensify his training again before the next year's marathon. The two began going their separate ways. Once when Jim—while doing his own workout—saw his former companion running, he suggested that they run together. His friend said he preferred to maintain his more leisurely pace. Jim tried to slow down to accommodate the other runner, but after a mile or two he gave up. The two men never ran together again.

Jim was unlike many other runners in that he rarely varied his workouts. It made him uncomfortable to modify his speed, which was why others not as well conditioned found it difficult to run with him. He also always ran the same eight miles a day rather than, as some did, alternating longer and shorter runs. Jim said that this was the distance that felt best to him, and thus it was the one he always preferred to run. His approach to running was based on the idea that it was imperative to go a sufficient distance. He admitted that he began each run doubting that he could finish it, and that he ran each day partly to convince himself he could make it.

Unfortunately, as the months went by and Jim continued running his eight miles every day, he began to have a number of orthopedic problems. The first symptom had actually appeared before the marathon, when his back had begun to hurt him. At that time he had consulted an orthopedic specialist, who prescribed a "muscle relaxant"—in fact, a tranquilizer. Although this solved the problem for a while, the pain in his back eventually returned, along with various problems in his legs. He went to the doctor several more times, each time receiving a new drug to counteract the latest strain on his body. Jim accepted the regular pain he now felt, saying that anyone who wanted to run the distances he did had to be prepared "to run through the pain."

As the next marathon approached, Jim looked forward to improving his time. About a month before the race, however, he developed a serious knee problem, one which the doctor he by now saw regularly said required complete rest for at least two weeks. Jim was in a quandary. He had just been planning to up his mileage again, and now this.

It was the roughest period Jim had faced since his divorce. He spoke to others only about his injury and its effect on his running. When he was not talking about running, he fantasized about it. As every workday came to a close, he thought hard about how he would spend his evening. He had gone to several films Diane had wanted to see now that his evenings were free but had barely been able to sit through them. He also found himself fidgeting throughout the day and had trouble getting to sleep. He was irascible and difficult to be with at other times.

All Jim could think about was that he was getting out of shape, and that he was losing his running edge. He joined a health club in order to swim, thinking that he could keep in shape this way. Paddling furiously through the water, he tried to develop a strenuous aerobic routine. But he could never get the same feeling as he did from running, and after ten days he went back to running. Two nights later, he had returned to his eight-mile-a-day workout. Just as he was about to finish running, his knee collapsed and—after he limped home—he had to be hospitalized. By this time Jim had been running for over four years. Running had become the most important thing in his life. He vowed to return to his regular running schedule as soon as possible.

how much is too much?

A running addiction. Jim's behavior was perhaps more extreme than that of most runners, but his reactions were not entirely different from those of many others who took up the exercise. Nearly all the people he introduced to running suffered at least one injury that kept them from running for a time and became a chronic problem when they started running again. But Jim was alone among his friends in not being able to hold off from running for even a short time, and in spending the time he was in agony from injuries preoccupied with ways to increase his running time. It is thus Jim who makes the clearest case for the addictive potential of running.

For Jim running was more absorbing than anything else. It provided him with a sense of gratification that his work did not, and which he was willing to endanger his personal relationships to attain. The appeal of the sensations engendered by running contrasted with the little that other things in his life seemed to offer Jim. For Jim, the joy of running consisted of its ability to erase all other concerns from his mind, and to allow him to enter a state of consciousness different from any other he experienced. He was not normally a relaxed person, though he had sought through many means—such as cigarettes, alcohol, eating, and relationships with women—to achieve relaxation. Running succeeded in accomplishing this for him in a way that nothing else had.

Jim's approach to his running showed a kind of drive and inflexibility not usually associated with the things people do for fun. He could not take running or leave it, he could not vary his running schedule to fit his mood or physical condition, and he could not modify his running style to suit the needs of others. When he was finally prevented from running by an injury, the structure of his life was in danger of crumbling.

It was the cumulative destructiveness of Jim's running habit that made its addictive nature clear. Originally, running was for Jim a way to increase his pride in himself and to improve his health. It gave him a new sense of what his body could do, and a new consciousness of himself. He never fully overcame his insecurities, however, and running eventually became a balm for his feelings of inadequacy. These feelings did not disappear; instead they were directed at running itself. Approaching each run, Jim felt a compulsive need to prove himself. He resumed running when his physical condition clearly indicated he should not. Jim's involvement with running had *not* made him more sensitive to messages from his body.

His willingness to sacrifice everything for the sake of running was destructive in a cyclical way. It was his lack of involvement with work and his neurotic style of dealing with others that made running seem so appealing. Ultimately, his running exacerbated these negative tendencies of his. This, combined with the fact that he continued to have doubts about himself as a runner and as a person, meant that the activity was having an overall negative impact on his self-esteem, and on his life in general.

A cost-benefit analysis. How does a person know when an activity is harmful? In some cases the answer seems simple, as when a person takes illicit drugs that are physically harmful and socially destructive. Actually, even here the problem is more complex. People take drugs because they derive some kind of reward from the experience. In order to understand the harmfulness of what they are doing, they must be able to see beyond the immediate gratification the drug provides.

The same holds for socially accepted activities, such as running. Again the major difficulty is motivating people to look beyond the short-term gratification the activity creates to evaluate its overall effect. The calculus of self-examination is emotional, not intellectual. We can, nevertheless, learn something about it by analyzing the different components of the impact an activity like running has on an individual, to see what this tells us about the cut-off point between healthy and unhealthy habits.

People generally run to improve their cardiovascular systems—to strengthen their hearts and increase the amount of oxygen circulated through the blood. This in turn increases their capacity for work, increases their sense of well-being, and decreases their likelihood of having heart attacks. Exercise also has orthopedic consequences. These include effects on the musculature, bones, and connective tissue of the body. Finally, at a commonsensical level, exercise requires time and energy. Considering these three aspects of exercise separately will help us assess the costs and benefits of the amount of running a person does.

Let us consider the cardiovascular effects of running first. There is evidence that after a point, the positive effects of running level off. A study of Harvard alumni found that the optimal amount of exercise for reducing the danger of heart attack was that which expended about 2,000 kilo calories a week. For the average man, this means about four hours of jogging. For someone who does a mile in, say, nine to twelve minutes, it means jogging five or six miles four times a week.* After this point, there was practically no further reduction in heart attacks.

Another study of jogging and running found an increase to almost double the number of injuries (knee and ankle injuries, shin splints, etc.) when subjects increased their running time from approximately 30 minutes a workout to 45 minutes. The increase in injuries was more than threefold when subjects kept the length of their workout constant at 30 minutes but increased the number of times they ran a week from three to five. The optimal amount of running from the standpoint of

*This mileage figure is inflated because it does not consider the amount of exercise a person gets through other means—walking, climbing stairs, or being active in other sports besides running. The study referred to (Paffenbarger et *al*., 1978) *did* find that strenuous sports like running, tennis, and skiing decreased the likelihood of heart attack more than the same expenditure of energy through light exercise would. What this issue opens up, of course, is whether an optimal level of exercise wouldn't combine different *types* of aerobic activity, a question we will deal with in later chapters.

figure 4.1.
The Impact of Running on an Average Individual.
Dotted lines suggest range for different individuals. Data in (a) are extrapolated from Paffenbarger **et al.** (1978). Data in (b) are based on Pollock **et al.** (1977).

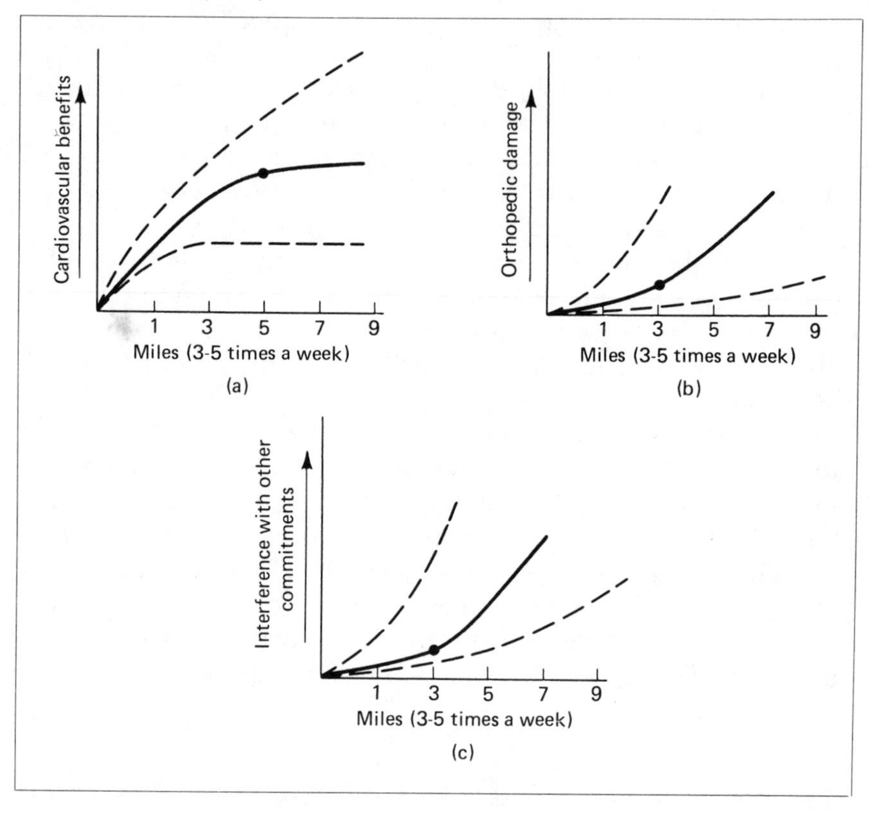

remaining injury free, according to this study, would be perhaps between three and four miles three or four times a week.

The expenditure of time and emotional energy is the hardest component of the running experience to evaluate for a point of diminishing returns. We would probably be no more arbitrary than we have been in other respects, however, if we said that devoting more than an hour-and-a-half or two hours to running would significantly disrupt a person's potential for engaging in other activities. The difference is between running which may be refreshing and running which begins to interfere, not only with the possibility of other extracurricular activities, but with family obligations and work. Considering the additional time needed for warm-up exercises and for showering and cooling off, an optimal investment of time in actual running might possibly be between half an hour and an hour several times a week and once over the weekend, or three to five miles three or four times a week.

There are, of course, individual differences. For example, someone with a runner's build—someone who is, say, 5′5″ tall and weighs 135 pounds—might easily run longer distances while escaping injury. For a hypothetical average person, however, the data above (represented by the curves in Figure 4.1) all point to the idea that there is an optimal amount of running. He will get the most benefits and suffer the least harm from running between three and five miles three to five times a week.

In addition to ignoring individual differences, the graphs in Figure 4.1 do not have real numerical values along their ordinates. It is impossible, really, to quantify the way running interferes with other activities and personal relationships and compare that figure to one expressing the physical benefits and damage caused by the same amount of running. Essentially, creating graphs such as these and juxtaposing them one upon the other is only possible for the individual himself or herself. For example, if a doctor has told someone that he needs to exercise more to avoid a heart attack, the advantages of running for that person would become more crucial. A runner who wants to experience the challenge of running a marathon would have to train harder for a given period. No one can decree, on an absolute basis, just when the disadvantages of something overcome the advantages. *However, it is the ability to be aware that such tradeoffs exist, and to be able to evaluate and compare the impact of an activity on the various aspects of one's life, which are the surest guarantees that one will not become immersed in an addiction.*

5 Growth and habits

Forming habits is a normal part of human behavior—nearly all of us sleep in the same place every night, go home to the same people, eat at the same time every day, and repeat activities we find enjoyable. We do not have enough time or energy to constantly evaluate basic aspects of our lives; we simply take them as givens. There is nothing wrong with this, and nothing addictive about it. If we refer to our definition of addiction, we find that it is a *pathological* habit, one that interferes with other activities and one that we cannot change no matter how much pressure we are under to behave differently. For example, we could say that a person who could never leave his home to work or to meet people was severely addicted to the reassurance of a familiar setting or routine. Even a habit which is required as a concomitant to daily life, such as eating, can be addictive.

The threat of death may be the ultimate test of an addiction. When told by a doctor that smoking will kill them, some people quit instantly and permanently. Others cannot do so. One woman who had had her jaw removed for cancer and who could not walk following the operation would crawl into a bathroom at the hospital to smoke, an act she could accomplish only by holding a cigarette to her lips with pincers.

Death often comes up in discussions of addictive love. Isn't despair at the death of a loved one a natural reaction? Yes, grief is normal. To mourn the loss of someone close to you whom you loved is as necessary as seeking love. But some people sacrifice their own lives at the death of another. They pine away, and quickly follow their mate to the grave.

Others, perhaps younger, devote their lives to the dead by filling themselves with guilt, or honoring one person's memory by ignoring everyone else. This is grief taken too far. Since killing oneself over an involvement or its cessation is undeniably harmful, the surest indication that what some call love is actually an addiction is when it results in death. Groups that work to prevent suicides, such as the Samaritans in Boston, report that the single largest impetus for attempted suicide is rejection by—or the disinterest of—a lover. Interviews with murderers indicate that the most frequent motive for killing is love. The victim may be the third party chosen by an unfaithful lover, or else the lover, husband, or wife himself or herself.

At the opposite extreme from habits that lead to physical injury and death are the habits that help us *combat* addictions and have a *positive* effect on our lives. How do we recognize these healthy habits, and how do we inculcate them in ourselves and others, such as our children? Much of the rest of this book deals with this central issue in the addiction field.

the criteria for healthy habits and involvements

A healthy habit is one that makes us feel better about ourselves, improves our ability to cope with challenges, helps us in our relationships with other people and activities, and enhances our enjoyment of life. We can approach the identification of such habits by reversing the criteria for addiction:

They expand awareness. Healthy activities increase our awareness of ourselves and our worlds. They do this by teaching us about our minds and bodies in the first place, and then by giving us the strength and ability to get outside ourselves to consider other things and other people. For example, running and other forms of exercise that get us in shape increase our knowledge of the needs and workings of our bodies. They give us a heightened sense of our physical selves that can then be translated into a greater sensitivity to external stimuli. A habit that is absorbing in this positive sense is one that requires our concentration for a time but gives us the energy to take an interest in other things as well.

In order to fulfill the criterion of expanding our awareness, relationships with individuals, groups, and organizations must not be so all-consuming that they blind us to all other individuals, groups, and organizations. On the contrary, a positive group involvement should teach us about people in general and therefore about how we can better relate to everyone.

One myth about enclosed groups or relationships is that they at least give the participants a stronger understanding of themselves and the people with whom they are in contact. This is not really so, since their interactions follow a pattern that fulfills the requirements of the group or the relationship, but does not allow them to show their true feelings or respond honestly to one another. For example, a relationship in which two people are forced to express their love at all times, and never criticize each other, teaches them nothing about themselves beyond their facades as lovers. On the other hand, a relationship with a person or a group that does not limit discussions or revelations along prescribed lines encourages the participants to be aware of different ways of looking at themselves.

They lead to other involvements. A healthy activity increases a person's confidence in his or her competence. Seeing that he can master one activity, a person realizes that he can master others that require the same abilities. A child who collects stamps sees that she can organize and categorize elements while studying or reading; a runner develops more control of his body and becomes more willing to dance on social occasions; a musician who brings pleasure to his audience anticipates pleasure from interactions with others.

They increase self-esteem. When a habit or an involvement causes a person to feel better about himself, that habit or involvement has healthy ramifications. However, the enhancement of the person's self-esteem that occurs must be cumulative; the person should not have to *return* constantly to the same activity to feel good about himself. His increased confidence and regard for himself must continue to be present when he turns his attention to other things.

In Jim's case, it was only when he was running that he felt good about himself, and even his confidence in his ability as a runner faded immediately when he was prevented from running for a day. On the other hand, consider the case of a woman who took ballet in order to develop grace and strength in her movements. In addition to acquiring specific physical skills, this woman came to *feel* more graceful and confident. The resulting changes in her posture and her disposition were apparent to everyone. She wasn't always able to continue taking dance lessons, but the change in her self-image that came about because of them was an enduring one, based on her knowledge that the side of her which was revealed in her dancing was a real and permanent part of her personality.

They bring pleasure. For an habitual activity to bring pleasure is the best guarantee that the habit has not progressed to a point where it controls the person, rather than vice versa. A person who does something because it is pleasurable is capable of evaluating why he is doing something, rather than simply acting compulsively. Thus a person who can sit down after dinner and concentrate on his enjoyment of the cigar he is smoking is not addicted. Nor can a person who actively savors the taste of the food he eats be addicted.

When an activity is enjoyable, it enlivens the person's life. The break the individual may have taken in his schedule to practice his habit, if it does nothing else, at least refreshes his senses. If a person looks forward to having lunch with someone because the interlude will be relaxing but stimulating, it can contribute to the person's capacity for carrying out his or her regular schedule even while having no direct effect on that schedule. Pleasure is a separate consideration from effective coping, yet the two can enhance each other.

They contain variety. Addiction is a static state of being; growth comes through exploring one's reactions to different phases of an activity. A healthy habit is many-faceted—it changes while the person is engaged in it. One type of change comes about when the person seeks to improve his mastery of an activity. This will mean becoming more aware of both the demands the activity makes on him and the rewards it can offer. He should not, in doing so, torture himself by disregarding evident physical and personal limitations, as Jim (the runner in the last chapter) did.

A good relationship, one that improves with time, is one in which the partners learn new things about each other and about themselves as the relationship proceeds. To accomplish this, two people must think new thoughts about themselves and each other, and be willing to communicate these thoughts to each other in ways each can accept and take in. Insights may come through participating together in new situations or interacting with new people, but this is not the only way in which they can occur. People can uncover new sides to themselves by approaching each other in new ways when they are alone, and by thinking seriously about each other when they are apart. Progress in relating to another person, like progress in any activity that is linked to personal growth, often takes place as a result of activities completely separate from the involvement.

other signs of healthful activities

What signs can a person look to to determine whether his habits are tending toward addiction or whether their impact is beneficial? Flexibility and the possibility of being sated are two keynotes of a healthy activity. If a person welcomes alternative experiences, or is capable of forsaking an activity when it would interfere with another worthwhile involvement, he is not a likely candidate for addiction. For example, if someone watches the news every evening because it keeps him well informed, rather than out of aimless habit, he will welcome other forms of intellectual stimulation that might prevent him from seeing the news on a given night. Too, when a person notes in himself the feeling that he has had too much of something, and has a desire to switch to some other form of entertainment, stimulation, or way of filling time, then the person may be fairly sure that his healthy decision-making impulses are still intact. Thus a woman who enjoys running may switch some evenings to playing tennis when a friend asks her to do so; and she will certainly want to change her running schedule when she begins to experience habitual pains as a result of her exercise.

When and if a person decides to leave aside an involvement for a time, he or she should be able to appreciate alternative activities for what they have to offer. Instead of regretting what he is missing, a person whose habits have been healthful will be capable of immersing himself in what is at hand. He will retain the conception that a risk is worth taking if there is a possibility of discovering a new and rewarding activity or relationship or some other benefit, rather than neurotically measuring anything new against what he has left behind. Spontaneity, then, is an important sign of healthful habits.

Finally, healthful activities not only feel good while they take place; they inspire a general sense of well being. It should not be necessary to defend such activities to oneself or one's friends, since their positive repercussions should be apparent. Healthful activities do not take away from a person's enjoyment of life, they magnify it. The fact that a habit has such an effect is the best evidence that it is the opposite of addiction.

a note on exceptionally gifted and motivated people

One issue that arises in evaluating healthfulness is drawing the line between addiction and dedication to activities which produce highly beneficial results for an individual or for society. Examples of the latter are often found in artistic endeavors and scientific discoveries. Actually, the criteria we have already developed apply here as well; there is no separate set of standards for gifted individuals. Some exceptional people do employ their talents in ways that increase their disabilities elsewhere, as in the interlocking cycles of the partial addiction in Figure 3.2, but such a circumstance is not a foregone conclusion. There are many people whose special talents or dedication in one area do not detract from their success in other areas of life, including their personal relationships.

The differences between addiction and an exceptional

degree of involvement in a healthy activity are evident in our criteria. People who are powerfully motivated to do well at an activity but are not addicted to it will show benefits outside the activity. They will not accept predictability as a characteristic of the activity but will strive for new experiences and goals. Finally, they will find their mastery of the activity pleasurable. Again, running provides a good case in point. William Morgan has compared world-class runners with other long-distance runners. His findings bear out our criteria remarkably well.

In the first place, elite runners have advantages deriving from their body types, athletic ability, and drive for excellence that place them on the outer limits of the curves in Chapter 4. The amount of time that is appropriate to devote to running is also greater for "professional" runners—those who derive their livelihood from the sport.

Many long-distance runners fantasize while running. Morgan calls this "dissociation." Elite runners, on the other hand, constantly monitor signals from their bodies and remind themselves of rules that improve their performance, such as "stay loose." This vigilance makes it far less likely that they will hurt themselves. The best runners dismiss the mythical wall of pain that supposedly appears during a marathon. As one such runner said, "I don't worry about pain zones or the wall. I try not to overextend myself. There really isn't pain for me—at least not until it's over."

Another runner reported, "There's no wall. The wall exists for runners who monitor their watches instead of their bodies." As a group, Morgan found, elite runners were looser and happier than other people. Obviously, such individuals are relating to their environments in a way that enhances their overall capabilities, their chances of success in running, and their mental and physical health. There is nothing here to suggest an addiction like that of the runner in the last chapter.

temporary addictions

There are some involvements that, although they bear some of the marks of addiction, are sometimes said to offer pathways away from addiction. The clearest examples are found among members of alcohol and drug treatment groups (and related groups such as those dealing with overeating, smoking, and gambling). Their commitment to such groups fulfills the criteria for addiction, but they view it as the best—or only—way to eliminate a particular unhealthy habit. Often these organizations (1) limit a person's serious contacts to those who share his problems and his approach to dealing with them; (2) teach a way of thinking that eliminates doubt and alternate conceptions; (3) provide a group identity and emotional support; (4) require regular attendance at meetings and strict conformity to rules; (5) pervade the person's life and protect and cushion the individual.

While according to the criteria for an addiction, these characteristics make membership in such groups indistinguishable from any other addiction, two additional aspects of involvement with such organizations must be evaluated to determine whether their claims to having therapeutic effects can be taken seriously. The first consideration is whether the negative impact of limiting a person's choices is outweighed by the beneficial impact of ceasing to use drugs or alcohol or removing some other habit. The second factor to be weighed is whether the control such groups have over an individual's life is temporary—that is, whether they are way stations on a path to greater individual integrity.

As in the case of any activity, making an assessment of such a group requires that a person measure a number of variables at the same time. A runner may increase his cardiovascular fitness while incurring orthopedic damage and lessening his ability to function when he is not running. The question is, at what point do the benefits of an activity cease to outweigh its negative effects? This must be an individual decision, because only the person concerned can attach a value to any component of the analysis. For example, a man who has lost his job or his family through gambling or drinking, or whose overeating or smoking has reached a point where it may kill him, may come to attach an importance to ceasing the activity that is destroying his life that transcends, for a time, every other consideration.

This does not mean that there are no other considerations to be evaluated in moving to eliminate a dangerous habit. People in some addiction-treatment groups, for example, may not only be allowed to develop other hazardous habits, they may be encouraged to do so. For example, some such groups are notorious for the amount of coffee consumed at their meetings, and the amount of cigarette smoke that hangs in the air there. What if a man protecting his liver from drinking develops lung cancer from smoking? The benefits here are obviously double-edged.

One disbenefit such groups often seem to take for granted is the absorption of the individual member's time and attention by the group at the expense of other meaningful activities and relationships. Here even more than in the substitution of one physically debilitating habit for another, equivalencies are hard to come up with. Limiting what a person can do, what he thinks and talks about, and whom he is comfortable with is not a negligible effect. Such a narrowing of focus is, after all, an essential element in the addiction cycle. Some people feel that this is too great a price to pay for modifying their habits. Thus they may seek alternate routes to accomplish this, routes that have their own pitfalls. Or they may decide that they will put up with the dangers of their bad habits if they feel these are necessary concomitants to other, healthy, sides of their lives. For instance, a doctor may prescribe drugs for himself that he knows are harmful if he depends on them for his equanimity, yet which enable him to continue a gratifying professional practice.

The crucial point in judging the benefits of involvement in a group is whether the involvement is an end in itself. If it is, it can be equivalent to the drug or other unhealthy habit it purports to cure. This is the danger of any group which claims that permanent membership in it is the only solution to the problem it is organized to combat. For example, Synanon, a West Coast organization that charters therapeutic communities for heroin addicts, has recently been accused of harrassing members to the point where their lives and health are endangered, of attacking those who wish to leave the community, and of assaulting critics of the organization. While some see these things as aberrations from the original policies of the group, in fact they are fairly natural conclusions of the addictive way in which the group has always been organized.

At the opposite extreme from groups like Synanon are those whose policy it is gradually to wean people away from the group as their main form of support. Instead of encouraging people to depend on the group's approval in order to function, such an organization nurtures its members' self-esteem so that they can cope with the outside world and thus develop sustaining rewards there. In stopping an addiction by working to expand members' horizons, the group defies the criteria for an addiction. This is a process which deserves to be called therapy.

6 Raising a nonaddicted child

When we consider the factors that contribute to addiction—social groups, culture and society, unpleasant or stressful situations, the individual's outlook and values—we find that some of them are more within our control than others. For example, it is usually easier to change particular situations than entire cultures or societies. This does not mean that it is not important to try for large-scale institutional change; but for most people the keys to combating addiction lie closer to home. For this reason, it is exceedingly important in preventing addiction to consider styles of child-rearing. No other single factor has as much impact on the rate of addiction in our culture. At the same time child-rearing is a matter most people confront personally in their lives.

The characteristics we have found to be related to addiction include the following: (1) fearfulness as a result of an exaggerated expectation of—and desire to avoid—pain, uncertainty, and failure; (2) a negative self-image and lack of confidence; (3) dependency stemming from an unwillingness to tackle problems directly, and a resulting desire to seek external solutions; and (4) an absence of the kind of values that promote psychological and physical health. These traits are worded here so that they readily suggest their opposites: (1) expectations of success from life combined with an ability to tolerate uncertainty and occasional failure; (2) good feelings about oneself and one's abilities; (3) an active orientation toward life and a sense of personal effectiveness; and (4) values that support sound psychological and physical functioning. All these traits are determined to a large extent by the experiences a child has at home, and secondarily by those he or she has in school and through other socializing institutions.

the value of experience

We have already noted that people often leave behind addictions when they mature. Adolescents who feel that the demands made on them exceed their capabilities are particularly susceptible to addictive experiences. As they become older and more able to cope with adult responsibilities, they have less need of protective mechanisms. On the other hand, some people may always have difficulty in assuming an adult role because their experiences have not prepared them adequately for adulthood.

Protection and independence. The only preparation for adulthood that makes sense is exposure during childhood to graduated experiences, experiences that allow the child to strive, to fail, and to succeed in achieving meaningful rewards. In one study of achievement motivation and fear of failure, a parent and a child were given a set of building blocks and instructions to construct something. Those children who had high fear of failure were those whose parents either took over the task of building entirely or who deprecated their children's efforts. Children who strove to achieve and found achievement rewarding had parents who provided encouragement and guidance without being overly critical and without giving such detailed instructions that the children did not experience success to be the result of their own efforts.

What most prevents parents from permitting a child to exercise judgment and to carry out tasks independently is parental fear—fear of injury to the child, fear that the child will not succeed, fear that the child will not perform as well as he or she would with a parent's direction. Bringing up a child involves a steady series of decisions about how much the child needs to be protected and how much he or she can do alone. An infant's first efforts to control his own movements by lifting himself up, leaning on objects, and standing and walking present these issues forcibly to a parent. Should the parent let the child try these movements without support? Should the parent allow the child to fail? Should the parent jump to cushion the impact of the fall? For parent and child, elemental experiences such as eating, dressing, going places, and thinking all create the same basic dilemma.

There is no easy way of resolving the conflict between a parent's need to protect his or her child and the child's need for independence. Every restriction placed on a child's self-management or his exploration of his environment has its effect on the child's evolving competence. Even knowing this, a parent may still consider it essential to shield or direct a child. Hopefully, protection will be offered or directions given with a consciousness of the balance of values that surround such choices. For let us consider what benefits the child derives from each independent foray into the world.

Often what the parent most fears—that the child will initially fail at a task—encourages the most learning. The child sees that to do something may take repeated efforts and that if he does not succeed immediately he may well do so eventually. More than this, the child begins to note the connection between making mistakes and correcting them. He learns to attend to feedback from his environment and his own experiences. Together, the attributes of being able to accept and build upon failure and of being sensitive to external and internal stimuli are strong bulwarks against addiction.

From the time a child reaches for a spoon to feed himself, we confront the ambivalence of being a parent. Will the child get enough nourishment this way? Even if he does, eating will certainly take longer and be messier. Yet the more often a child has a chance to regulate what he does and what he takes in, the more able he will be to decide for himself how much is too much, and how much is appropriate. Underlying this ability is a sense a child develops that he controls relevant parts of his environment and hence what happens to him. Here again there is a strong relationship between attitudes toward child-rearing and the attitudes that support or prevent addiction in the adolescent or adult.

School, achievement, and nurturance. Historically our culture has always stressed achievement; in recent years, however, a certain ambivalence has developed about it. One of the sternest warnings parents hear now is not to push their children too hard. Yet we saw in Chapter 2 that both the pursuit of achievement and its opposite—the avoidance of challenges out of fear of failure—are important for reasons other than succeeding in school. Often when people talk about demanding too much from a child, what is really involved is insufficient grounding for the child to decide for herself what she will do and how she will do it. One woman who had striven hard to get a Ph.D. while she already held a job as a teacher had two teenage daughters. Her husband, who was a lawyer, took a laissez-faire attitude toward his children's achievement. The mother, on the other hand, had high aspirations for her offspring. Ultimately, one of the daughters dropped out of college and became a heavy drug user; the other got a degree but decided to get married rather than continue her education. For her, college had been a constant source of anxiety, and it was with relief that she left it behind.

People who knew the family took the daughters' behavior as evidence that if one demands too much from children they will rebel. In fact, while the mother did emphasize that good marks were important, she did little else to pass along her own values to her daughters. She herself believed that accomplishment, outside interests, intellectual stimulation, and self-reliance were also important. Yet she often got nervous when her daughters suggested projects they would like to try. When one asked to paint her room and showed the mother a model she had made of how it would look, the woman put the model aside to show relatives while rejecting the plan itself. When her children asked for help with school assignments, something they did increasingly as they grew older, her efforts to help them were often frenzied. She became depressed and anxious as she compared the deficient work the children showed her with her hopes that they would perform exceptionally. As a result, the one daughter became listless and dependent on her mother's prodding and suggestions. The other daughter took her mother's dreams of a college education to heart, but never really felt the desire to learn things or to excel intellectually.

The woman in this story was not the monster that the phrase "pushing too hard" suggests; in fact, it was her obvious concern and support for her children that made their internal conflicts so great. What the woman did not see, for all her wish to encourage her children, was that the desire to achieve grows out of a whole style of interaction, and not just from scrutinizing homework and report cards. Those parents who foster a striving for achievement in their offspring are actually those who sometimes ignore their children's requests for help and instead encourage them to do as much as possible on their own.

Among other things, this conveys to the children the parents' belief in them, which in turn builds their belief in themselves—another counterweight to addiction. Achievement-fostering parents are also more likely to respond to achievement in their children and to reward it whenever it appears. This nurturing attitude expresses itself in the parents' encouragement of the infant's mastery of such skills as walking, talking, and feeding itself more than it comes out as a wish for the child simply to do well at school.

As our culture and the individuals within it continue to feel ambivalent about such goals as being successful, doing well at school, and making money, there is a tremendous potential for gaps between what a child has been prepared to accomplish and what he is asked to do. It is these discrepancies that are often at the heart of addictions not only among those who fail to achieve, but among those apparently successful people who perpetually doubt whether they are as successful as they seem to others. The internal stress the person experiences in either case is one which addiction is all too ready to relieve.

The child who is most likely to avoid addiction is one who has an absorbing interest in some activity at which he or she can excel. It makes no difference what relationship this activity has to schoolwork or to the parents'—or even the child's—ultimate plans. It is valuable in itself if it gives the child a chance to decide to do something, to persevere, to accomplish what he or she has set out to do, and to feel sure and good about his or her relationship to the world.

Educational experiences. When children could explore their environments, learn what they needed to know to survive and flourish, and develop confidence in themselves and their worlds purely through the natural flow of their lives, addiction was not so likely to occur. Today, children are isolated for the purpose of education. Their efforts in school produce nothing that is usable beyond the school's boundaries, and they feel unable to make real contributions to their own or others' lives. The setting in which they spend much of their time is an artificial one in which teachers teach and children learn, and where the time, place, and materials are set apart from those of the actual worlds of work and play.

In the city of Calgary, in the province of Alberta, Canada, a group of people within the school system have organized a program they call Can Do. Their aim in this program is to incorporate into the curriculum activities that expose children to the materials, opportunities, and experiences present in real-world endeavors. For example, a take-apart lab offers the children obsolete or broken electronic equipment to investigate. Children make ice cream, build things, use tools, and initiate, organize, and discuss their efforts. Through such activities, they learn that they can have a genuine impact on their surroundings—that they can produce useful things and that they can play a role in deciding what they should do and how they should proceed. As students master some of the skills and tools that are available, the staff helps them to make more significant investments of time and effort in activities and to stretch the abilities they are developing. The children see how progress is made through advance and failure. They also learn about collaborative relationships with other people, peers and teachers both. Instruction is made so much more sensible by the relevance of the immediate experiences about which teachers and students are talking.

This educational program teaches all the qualities—the independence, competence, and respect for oneself and others that come from experiencing failure and success, affecting one's environment, and directing one's own efforts—that a child or an adult needs to combat addictive tendencies. These same qualities can also be promoted by activities and attitudes in the home. In truth, this kind of education is perhaps best viewed as a family responsibility. In building defenses against addiction, parents can and should be their children's best educators.

nonaddictive values and outlooks

Seeing the world as a reasonable place. People seek addictive experiences when they feel unable to cope realistically. Their attitude stems partly from their feelings about themselves, and partly from their view of the world. Some people see the world in an unreasonable light: either they believe that it is irrational and that it will not respond to systematic effort to change any part of it, or they believe that it is—or *should* be—a source of womblike security. A view of the world that works better than either of these is one that sees the world as working according to certain principles—principles that can be learned and mastered—but also as a place where success is not achieved without some effort.

How does an individual evolve one view of the world as opposed to another? The first—and perhaps most important—world that all of us learn about is that presided over by our parents. The environment parents arrange for a child is a primary source of the notions he or she will have of the way the universe works. The main dimension of this universe with which we are concerned from the standpoint of addiction is its responsiveness. Some children learn that, when they make an appropriate effort, they will get the reaction they desire. Others learn that the world is not interested in them, and that it is hard to make an impression on one's surroundings. Finally, some children learn that their environment is so completely aware of and responsive to them that all they need do is wish for something and it will occur.

One study of developing competence in the first three

years of life found, by observing mothers with their children, that there were certain optimal amounts and kinds of attention given to children. The children who developed best according to the criteria of the researchers were those whose parents were nearby and ready to respond, but who only occasionally did so. When the children became enthusiastic, frustrated, or curious about something, they would turn to an adult to share these feelings. The parents of the well-developed children would respond quickly by teaching them something about the situation, by removing insurmountable barriers the children had encountered, or by making some other appropriate response. At times, the parents injected a note of reality by indicating that they were busy and could not respond immediately. All the interactions that took place between the well-developed children and their parents throughout the day took up no more than 10 percent of the children's waking time. What the researchers found to be most important about these interactions was that the children initiated them.

Not surprisingly, disinterest in or unawareness of a child's activities on the part of parents or supervising adults produced poorer results for the children. A perpetual readiness to respond to a child also had important drawbacks as a child-rearing style. Children whose parents dropped everything the moment the children showed signs of wanting attention learned to depend exclusively on adults to remove obstacles, rather than attempting to explore solutions on their own.

Herein we see the genesis of addictive and nonaddictive outlooks. Children who see that the world responds to them randomly, if at all, learn to be fatalistic and to accept being controlled by outside forces. They do not believe it pays to struggle to assert their will. Oddly, children whose environments have been the opposite of insensitive—whose parents have reacted to their needs almost before they themselves recognized them—are also disinclined to take an active stance toward their surroundings. They cannot wade through situations where uncertainty or complexity interferes with the immediate gratification of their needs.

It is children who view the world as an orderly and manageable place, who believe that making an effort is worthwhile, and who feel that their actions make a difference who will not have an addictive outlook as adults. Such people believe that what happens to them can be traced back to reasonable causes. Should they have a problem, they will look for its sources and work to modify these. They have neither the passivity or "learned helplessness," nor the desire for quick, easy, magical solutions, that are the hallmarks of addiction.

Attitudes toward health, moderation, and self-regulation. Being able to use a drug moderately requires balancing other values and needs against the use of that drug. This in turn means having other things besides the drug in one's life that are important and knowing other people besides drug users with whom one wishes to associate. A person's appreciation of people and activities stems from his or her whole perspective toward life: is it viewed fearfully or as a source of positive opportunities and pleasure? A person's faith in the world affects all of his involvements along with his likelihood of being addicted. It is also something parents have a large hand in creating, first by training children to accept challenges and to feel they can handle them, and second by giving children a sense that the world is a positive and welcoming place.

Parents can give children this sense in a number of ways. They can show that they enjoy doing things themselves. They can encourage children to try things and lead them to anticipate good outcomes when they do. They can speak optimistically about life and the work, play, and people that comprise it. Most of all, they can make it clear that they themselves do not seek escape and oblivion as an alternative to being alive.

One natural way parents can do this is by controlling their own use of drugs and other substances. Children learn moderation by example. This is especially true with respect to the use of legal drugs, such as alcohol and cigarettes. A parent's compulsive smoking makes it likely that a child too will be a cigarette addict. The offspring of alcoholics or those who abuse alcohol are also more likely to drink to excess.

But alcoholic parents are not the only ones who increase their children's disposition to be alcoholics. Abstemious parents and groups are also more likely to produce alcoholics than controlled drinkers. What is absent when parents do not drink is a positive model for children of the social uses of drinking. In addition, abstemious parents often overstate the dangers of drinking so severely that they convince their children that a person's reaction to alcohol is beyond his or her control. When their children do drink, this then becomes a self-fulfilling prophecy. The disease theory of alcoholism offers a similar portrait of the effects of alcohol, and thus it too can be said to contribute to an outlook that fosters addiction.

Emphasizing how much a person should *not* do something may, on the other hand, create a pathological reaction against the activity. *Anorexia nervosa*—where people strive so compulsively to be thin that they actually endanger their health—is an example of this. One woman developed an anorexic condition as a teenager. Later in life she was able to overcome the compulsion to starve herself, although she would always be preoccupied with weight and weight control. She reported that, as a child, she had been very active. Yet her parents, both of whom had been obese themselves and had successfully lost weight as adults, continually reminded her not to eat as much as she wanted to. In this way they destroyed her natural ability to regulate her intake and expenditure of calories. Frightened as she was of becoming fat, her only solution was a perpetual near-starvation diet.

A series of studies have shown that obese people are not capable of sensing their bodies' actual need for food, and that they rely on external signs to tell them when they should eat and when they should cease eating. Relying on indicators like the smell of food or the amount of food on the table causes them to eat too frequently or too much. Not being tuned in to internal hunger states, as the anorexic women was not, forces a person to rely on external devices, such as a general prohibition on eating, to resist overeating.

All addictions involve failures in the individual's self-regulating mechanisms. The greatest protection against such failures is a sure sense of self. Trust in one's own feelings is taught by parents who convey a respect for the child's knowledge of his own needs, and who are convinced that *no outside force can damage the child more than lack of self-respect and self-reliance.*

7

Rooting out addictions

The many mistaken and costly ideas about defeating addiction that have been propagated all stem from the same fundamental error. This is the failure to understand that a person is addicted to an experience. If a cure for addiction fails to take into account a person's need for the addictive experience, he or she will simply be set loose to seek a comparable experience elsewhere. Early in the century, when heroin addicts were deprived of a legal supply of the drug, they turned in large numbers to alcohol. It provided them with a similar experience, and many became alcoholics. Today, various government agencies have documented the fact that when heroin is scarce, addicts readily turn to barbiturates, alcohol, and sedatives.

Methadone maintenance is one example of this wrongheaded approach to combating addiction. It is the most popular type of heroin addiction treatment program in the United States and most narcotic addicts are exposed to it at one time or another. Yet its founders, Drs. Dole and Nyswander, note that methadone maintenance's impact has been minimal "at best."

Many people continue to use a narcotic while taking methadone. What is more, there is now a wide black market for methadone. For some addicts, methadone is not an adequate substitute for heroin because it does not provide the same experience. So they continue using the street drug. Those for whom the methadone experience is an adequate substitute find the drug so attractive that they may *prefer* it to heroin.

A similar substitution of one addiction for another occurs when a person alternates between overeating and smoking. Or, a person who gives up drinking may form an addiction to a pharmaceutical substance such as Valium, start to smoke heavily, or drink large quantities of coffee. At a more subtle level, we saw in Chapter 5 how membership in a group organized to combat addiction can itself be addictive if it limits participants to one lifestyle, one set of associations, and one way of thinking and feeling.

In all the cases above, a person—or society—may decide to make the trade-off between one addiction and another. There may be benefits from taking a drug in a legal, supervised methadone program in which the addict is available for therapy. Or a person may wish to smoke rather than be overweight or addicted to an intoxicating drug—such as alcohol—that hinders daily functioning. But these pros and cons do not in any way change the basically addictive nature of the involvement the person has formed. This is especially true when the replacement addiction is harmful in its own right, as smoking and caffeine consumption are.

If a person's need for the addictive experience is not attacked directly, no program can have any long-term success. In the place of successful treatment many people form lifetime commitments to a group or a type of therapy. Only while the person is in a program or in therapy can he or she resist the pull of the drug and the experience it produces. Away from the program, the person is immediately drawn back into his or her

figure 7.1.
Breaking the Addiction Cycle.
Addiction short-circuits a person's achievement of real-world rewards through normal functioning. Therapy must remove the barrier presented by an addiction so that a person can experience these real rewards. One way for therapy to do this is to provide intermediate rewards that lead to realistic action.

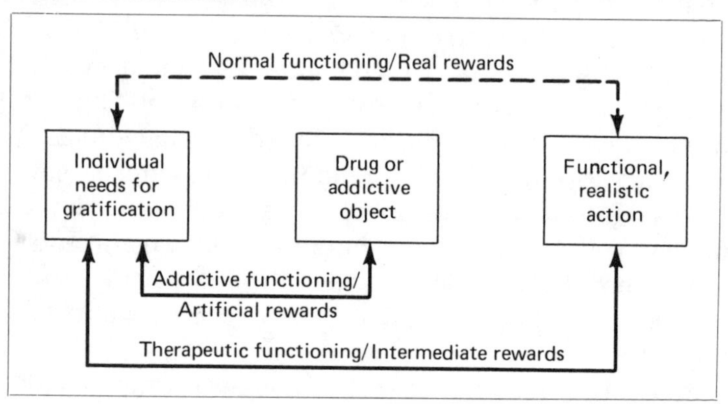

old patterns, no matter how long the intervening period of abstinence from the drug has been.

replacing rewards from addictive experiences

People return to an addictive experience because they find the experience rewarding. The rewards are, however, double-edged. One of the hallmarks of an addiction is that its overall impact is negative. This makes the rewards it provides that much more alluring. Suppose a woman takes tranquilizers to combat anxiety. Since she has not done anything about the sources of her anxiety, she feels more tension when the tranquilizer wears off and has a *greater* need for the drug. This is the nature of the addiction cycle.

All meaningful addiction counseling begins with an understanding of the function the addiction serves for the addict, and the rewards the person seeks from the addiction. From the addict's standpoint, the benefits of exchanging the known—if damaging—results of the addiction for the promised—but uncertain—rewards of a "straight" life are highly problematic. It is all well and good to be told that one will be able to handle the pressures of work and family. But the addict *knows* that he or she can count on alcohol, pills, food, or an injection for immediate gratification.

One of the main ways any therapy for addiction operates is by providing intermediate rewards that substitute for the rewards from the addiction until a person is capable of garnering real-world gratifications. Thus a work-training program may pay a person while he trains in order to encourage him to persist until he can earn a paycheck from a regular employer. Or consider a woman who is grossly overweight. Even should she eat properly for a day, or a week, she will still be fat. Perhaps her weight will have dropped from 286 pounds to 279. What, then, is going to keep her eating in a moderate way?

The woman may hope that, at the end of a long process, her weight will be normal, she will be able to participate in physically demanding activities, she will be attractive to others, and she will have more energy. In the meantime, she must obtain sufficient rewards from her food-restricted life to continue trying to lose weight. Methods for obtaining such rewards are as varied as the preferences people have for different kinds of rewards. Many people find the emotional support of groups such as Weight Watchers to be highly effective. The whole group notes the smallest progress made by a participant and cheers the individual on toward continued progress. Other people may get needed help from a therapist who can tell them how well they are doing, and who reminds them of the goal they are seeking to attain. Still others, those with the determination and ability to lose weight independently, may be rewarded sufficiently by successively lower readings on a bathroom scale which indicate that the goal is slowly being approached. The nature of addiction is such, however, that very few seriously addicted people can manage without structured support. This is the reason, as addictions increase, for the proliferation of addiction-fighting groups and therapies.

treating groups as objects of change

There is another type of group support that is rarely tried in our society. It involves not the formation of groups on the basis of common addictions, but the use of existing units such as the family or work group. Efforts are made to produce healthy changes in the group as a whole to create a support network for change for each individual within the group. For example, in a normal work organization there is a good chance that a number of people will be having problems with their weight, blood pressure, and consumption of cigarettes, coffee, or other drugs. If everyone takes part together in a program to eliminate unhealthy habits and to fill the vacuum with healthy group activities, such as calisthenics at lunchtime, there is a much greater likelihood that any single individual will follow a new, healthful regimen. Each person's efforts serve as a reminder of the common goal and as a stimulus for all to try to achieve it. In some cases a group goal is established, such as a certain total weight loss or reduction in the number of cigarettes smoked daily by the group. Families and social groups, too, can consciously work to change their overall eating habits, to exercise more as a group, or to encourage as many people in the group as possible to quit smoking. Or they can focus their attention on one "target" individual whose difficulties are especially severe. Whether working together on common problems or the problems of one person among them, friends and kin can serve as "therapists" for one another.

All may not be so rosy within a family or work group, of course. Forces at home or at work at least as frequently point people towards addictions as away from them. Stress is one such factor in groups that not only leads to addiction, but is independently related to heart attacks, high blood pressure, and digestive tract ailments such as ulcers. For the individual in a group, stress may result from the person's role in the group, from the type of work he does, from the climate of the organization as a whole, or from the personalities of the people on the job. Sometimes nothing short of large-scale organizational change (or, in a family, divorce) may be effective in lessening stressful factors.

One method which stops short of a complete group overhaul is increasing communication among people in the group so that they can express what is troubling them and understand better what is on one another's mind. Sensitivity groups may attempt this for people who have never met before, or who are cohorts in an ongoing organization. Family therapy also looks at psychological problems as a symptom of the whole group, in this case the family, and tries to break down unhealthy patterns of interaction among family members. Despite the complicated nature of group and organizational processes, it is safe to state that the increase in communication among members of any social unit is the single largest step a group can take to reduce pressures leading to unhealthy behavior.

changing social affiliations

Unfortunately, it is not always possible to get an entire group—or a mate—to go along with the changes one wants to make. In fact, social ties are often the greatest barriers to changing behavior. An individual's habit may be necessary for the stability of a relationship or a group. For example, for one member of a group suddenly to announce that he feels he and his friends are drinking too much is an invitation for that person to be rejected by the group. Or, take a man whose drinking has been a problem for many years. While a therapist may wonder how the man's wife has been able to tolerate his unreliability and abusiveness, in fact she may depend on her husband's weakness to give her a hold over him. We have already seen how she herself may be addicted to her role as an alcoholic's wife.

As a result, although therapy may instill in an addict some desire to change, his mate or his acquaintances can draw him back to his old habits. One man had a massive heart attack in his fifties. In the hospital he lost a great deal of weight. His doctor had told him that keeping the weight off was a life-and-death matter. However, when he returned home, his wife began encouraging him to eat as he had in the past. His enjoyment of her cooking made her feel appreciated. She could also have been frightened by the prospect of a newly-thin, attractive mate. Within the year the man had another massive coronary that killed him.

In cases like this, where a mate, a friend, or a group of friends encourages the abuse of drugs or alcohol, overeating, gambling, or unwholesome interpersonal relationships, a person may be forced to sever his old connections. Only by taking such action may he be able to break the destructive habit. In this way, hopefully, he is making a positive choice about the kind of person he wants to be through establishing new relationships with people and groups whose values he admires and wishes to emulate.

changing habits, outlooks, self-concepts, and values

All addictions are habitual responses to situations, situations that foster anxiety and fear which the addiction assuages for a time. Removing an addiction requires replacing this mode of responding with more functional responses—actions that *alle-*

viate the person's anxieties and problems. One reason combating addiction is so difficult is that it is usually necessary to eliminate reactions to familiar stimuli, reactions that have been repeated and ingrained for periods often approaching decades. Whenever certain stimuli or situations present themselves, all aspects of the person's being are predisposed to respond in the way to which his body and mind have become accustomed. While these learned responses are incredibly indelible, a technology for changing such behavior patterns has been developed. We will turn to this technology in the next chapter.

Underlying an addict's patterned responses to a set of stimuli is an overall outlook and relationship to the environment that favors addiction. This outlook, as we have seen, is defensive. It anticipates defeat, and sees the environment as an alien and unmanageable place. To change, an addict must alter his view of the world to the point where he feels comfortable in his surroundings, and confident of his ability to deal with them. The most important element enabling someone to make such a shift is enhanced self-esteem, when a person comes to feel that he is a match for the demands he will face. In some ways the development of a more positive self-concept is a natural consequence of the behavior modification techniques we shall explore. But it is not a necessary consequence. A person must be helped to draw together the changes in his habits that occur to form a concept of the new person he wishes to be.

In addition to changing his outlook and self-concept, the addicted person needs to modify his values and attitudes. We have already seen what some of these key attitudes are. A person has to want to be healthy, to believe that he *deserves* to be healthy. What is more, he has to feel that health is within his grasp—that he can achieve it by his own actions. As long as a person chooses to believe that his health—or lack of it—is a result of outside forces, he will never feel that he has permanent control over the behavior that promotes health.

What does all this mean to an addicted person? An obese person may begin to change her style of eating and thus make a dent in her body weight. Yet instead of feeling better about herself and seeing herself in a new light, she may conceive of herself as an inveterate problem eater who will always be unattractive. Obviously, this attitude undermines any progress she has made. To continue to diet successfully she must start to think of herself as a person who can be thin. She must convince herself that, by maintaining proper eating habits, she can make her life more fun, widen her circle of friends, and increase the scope of her activities. She must substitute these rewards—or the thought of them—for the quick and easy gratification she has been accustomed to receiving from overeating. Feeling well and having a healthy self-image will then be a natural outgrowth of the improvements in her eating habits.

dealing with the world beyond an addiction

There are no easy cures for addiction. Being firmly ensconced at the opposite end of the addictive spectrum—and not just simply biding one's time until inertia and the weight of the past pull one back into one's old ways—means forming a new relationship with the world. To be able to discard an addiction and the gratifications from that experience, one must be able to approach normal experiences without fear. To succeed, therefore, addiction therapy must confront the weaknesses in a person's ability to cope and the anxieties they cause.

For people who have been prevented from acquiring basic life skills, addiction therapy may include learning to be on time, to express one's feelings and intentions in understandable language, and to react to untoward events calmly and effectively. People in therapy programs may need to be taught specific job skills—or to translate abilities they already have into marketable skills. For some people, like the man who is only an alcoholic at home, the workaholic, or the person addicted to a mate or lover, the skills that need to be strengthened are those having to do with intimate relationships. Understanding one's feelings, recognizing and controlling unhealthy impulses toward other people, and attracting attention and appreciation in nonfrantic but effective ways are the life skills these kinds of addicts have failed to develop.

An addiction is not an isolated phenomenon, and at least as much attention has to be given to the context of an individual's problem as to the harmful habit itself. Otherwise pressures in the world outside the therapist's office will drive the person back to his addiction as surely as they led him to it in the first place. With this in mind, we may turn to what we know about breaking habits.

8
The technology of habit control

Although for a time many people looked to Freud and his descendants for definitive methods for correcting behavior, the dominant influence of psychiatric therapy has long since faded. At first, Freudian psychology was optimistically challenged by the first generation of behaviorists—practical men, from Pavlov to Skinner, whose theories had evolved from experimental psychology. Yet they quickly joined psychoanalysts as the butt of literary jokes before they were able to demonstrate any superior ability to produce the changes they sought in human beings. Along with the efficacy of their methods, *their right* to decide the ends toward which people's behavior should be directed was challenged.

the age of behavior modification

Today many people seek to change themselves. There is general concern about self-improvement, generally meaning psychological rearrangement. At the same time a new group of behaviorists has appeared with a set of modest but practicable techniques for helping people help themselves. Their methods have now been turned into something like a mass production industry.

One reason behavior modification and its proponents have become so popular is the continued lack of success of in-depth analysis in dealing with easily identifiable problems such as smoking and overeating. It is rare now to encounter someone who would seriously suggest to a person that he or she see a psychiatrist for help in quitting smoking or losing weight. In fact, the entire history of efforts to change people's behavior has inspired a guardedness about the prospects for ultimate success from any given technique. Recognition of this difficulty is a gauge of the reputability of a program. In judging such programs I use what I call a 90 percent rule. Any program that claims it is 90 percent successful is a fraud.

Exactly how well do behavior modification techniques work? In dealing with long-term problems such as overeating, alcoholism, and smoking, the best programs measure success rates of between 30 and 70 percent a year after treatment. The percentage of graduates of such programs who have licked their bad habits *permanently* is probably considerably smaller, since the number of successful clients tends to shrink with each successive measurement.

What about those organized groups, such as Alcoholics Anonymous and Weight Watchers, which regularly claim higher success rates? Such programs weight their assessments so much in their favor that it is practically impossible to extrapolate a realistic estimate from their figures. For example, there is typically no follow-up of people who attend one or a few meetings and then disappear from the group. Also, those who continue to come but have periodic relapses are counted as successes. Thus the second Rand study of alcoholism found that, for the heavy drinkers typically referred to federal treatment programs, "alcoholics who regularly attend AA are not more likely than others to be free of serious alcohol problems later." (This quote from the researchers themselves, it should be noted, is in contradistinction to the National Institute on Alcohol Abuse and Alcoholism press releases, which attempted to show the AA treatment to be superior. See page 31.)

Objective follow-up studies indicate that the best nonbehavioral treatment programs for drinking, smoking, and overeating have success rates of from 10 to 20 percent. Some programs have been found to have had no impact, and others have actually had *negative* effects. We might also examine here the results of drug treatment programs. Again, since organizations frequently develop their own impressions of how well they are doing, it is often hard to know for certain how much good is being accomplished. One large-scale measurement of drug treatment results occurred under the auspices of New York State's Narcotic Addiction Control Commission. The program in question was a residential treatment program managed largely by medical specialists. Of the 5172 people who entered the program, 141 were drug-free at the end of eighteen months. Thus the program had a cure rate of 3 percent.

Against this backdrop, behavior modification programs, even with their often considerable limitations, appear in a much more favorable light. As a result, the distinctions between behavioral and nonbehavioral approaches have grown less clear. The usefulness of many behavioral techniques has become so commonly acknowledged that any program would be likely to incorporate them. (Alternately, one might say that some techniques are so *obvious* that it is ridiculous to give them the label "behavioral.") In any case, the best programs of a behavioral type have become more and more inclusive and eclectic. Rather than being dogmatic or highly theoretical, practitioners comb the field for techniques that work, and when they find one in the literature or in practice, they simply include it in their treatment.

The result is a remarkable commonality of techniques that, while not infallible, have an impact on a tremendous range of problems. These include such apparently unrelated behaviors as smoking, overeating, problem drinking, and drug abuse, as well as compulsive television viewing, gambling, worrying, and even behavior patterns that surface in sexual or love relationships. Thus there are groups that follow the example of AA in dealing with peoples' difficulties in intimate relationships. The underlying similarities in these various realms of behavior have helped point toward the unified conception of addiction and healthy and unhealthy habits that this book presents. In turning to treatment methods that have come from behavior modification and therapy, we shall again encounter many of the themes we have touched on in earlier chapters. Foremost among these is the idea that there is no clear line of demarcation between a bad habit a person wishes to lose and an addiction that dominates a person's life.

tools for controlling addiction

Self-examination and keeping records. A standard ingredient of successful addiction programs is the records clients are asked to keep of when, where, and how much food, cigarettes, or alcohol they have consumed. These bare facts may be the first inescapable evidence of their addictive patterns. Such records also give people some indication of the kinds of situations that cause them to resort to their addictions. For example, people may discover that they invariably drink too much at social gatherings, or that they always smoke when they get on the phone, or when they have to interact with people—such as a boss or a parent— with whom they have a sensitive relationship. Looking at the normal cycle of their days, people find that there are predictable points of boredom, tension, or habit where they unthinkingly engage in the behavior they wish to avoid.

Some people are able to alter their behavior on the basis of this raw information alone. More often, it is a stimulus to begin the process of recognizing and coping with problems—a process addiction has short-circuited. Moments of anxiety, boredom, or desperation are clues that tell therapy clients and those helping them what the clients fear or cannot deal with. This inaugurates a therapeutic process of learning to handle emotional impulses that have become unmanageable—for example, by asking what there is about a given relationship with a particular person which makes it so painful that it leads the person to smoke, drink, or overeat.

Breaking addictive links. Recording the circumstances in which addictive behavior occurs works because it is one way of enabling people to gain control over a response that has become automatic in certain situations. There are other techniques to break down this connection, and to give people behavioral options. As we have mentioned before, cigarette smokers may be asked to rate the enjoyment they anticipate from a cigarette on a scale from one to ten before they smoke. This serves the purpose of alerting some people to the fact that smoking is not really pleasurable for them. Carrying the procedure further, clients then learn to evaluate an habitual action for its benefits before they carry it out. For example, smokers may be instructed not to light up unless the pleasure they anticipate from a smoke is worth at least a four (subsequently to be raised to five, six, and so on).

Rating scales are one way of introducing a pause before an action during which people may consider what they are about to do. Another way to break an automatic link between a situational stimulus and an addictive response is to *forbid* the behavior in certain circumstances. For example, suppose a person has noted that he or she always nibbles food or smokes at a certain spot in the house. That spot may be made off bounds for the habit—a person may be allowed to eat anywhere but in the living room, drink anywhere but in the kitchen, and so on. An opposite but equivalent approach is to limit the target behavior to just one spot in the house: to allow a person to eat *only* in the kitchen, or smoke or drink in one chair and nowhere else.

Eliminating tempting stimuli. The evocative power of certain stimuli is particularly difficult for an addicted person to handle. A sensible program for revamping eating behavior will therefore recommend not keeping snack food around or putting it at the back of shelves, out of sight. There are limits to how much people can control what they are exposed to as a way of controlling their behavior, however. Mario Lanza's manager, for example, may have been a bit extreme in locking him in his hotel room to prevent him from overeating. (The manager was also unsuccessful.) Yet, at least in one's own house, curtailing temptation can be a sound policy. Some people find that they can only limit their TV viewing by getting rid of their sets. Most people could reduce the amount of time they and their children spent watching television if they simply put the set in an out-of-the-way room. This is one example of how a policy that makes sense for a fully addicted individual can be modified to be helpful to the more typical activity overuser or abuser.

Moderating excessive responses. One of the larger-than-life issues in the addiction field is whether alcoholics can ever hope to drink moderately. The pressure created by ingrained habits and responses is so great that a behavior pattern often feels predetermined and immutable. Thus, people who have difficulty regulating their intake of food must usually struggle all their adult lives against excessive eating patterns.

As for whether an alcoholic can learn to take in smaller amounts of alcohol, consider the following pieces of research. In one study, forty advanced ("gamma") alcoholics were given flavored drinks, half of which contained alcohol. Half of those receiving the beverage with alcohol in it and half of those not receiving alcohol were *told* they were getting alcohol. Those who were told that they had had liquor were more likely to request an additional drink, regardless of whether they had *actually* had any alcohol. We see that the *idea* people have that they can't control themselves once they've had a drink *leads* to loss of control. On the other hand, there was no evidence in this study that the alcohol itself led to a desire for more alcohol. Another experiment indicates that a general tendency toward overconsumption—one could even call it gluttony—can underlie what is called alcoholism. In this study alcoholics were shown to drink more of *whatever* fluid they were given, whether or not it contained alcohol.

Addicts fail to evolve moderate responses to a substance or a situation for any number of reasons: in some cases parents or other important role models do not set an example of moderation; in other cases the addicts learn excessive patterns that seem natural and inescapable from those who initiate them into the activity; and in still other instances addicts are driven to expand their usage patterns to excessive levels by problems for which the addictive activity offers a palliative experience. Many programs have successfully demonstrated that it is possible to teach addicts to moderate formerly excessive behavior. For example, compulsive overeaters may be instructed to set their forks down after every bite of a meal. Addicted overeaters and drinkers both may be given a set amount of time before which they may not finish a portion of food or a drink. In this way, an overeater can learn not to gobble food and an alcoholic can learn to sip a drink. Or alcoholics may simply learn to limit the number of drinks they have at a sitting. Treatment succeeds when people develop an idea of what it means to partake of a substance in moderation, and no longer require artificial limits to guarantee that they do not exceed healthy boundaries.

Avoiding surrendering to the addiction. There is a crucial point in the addiction cycle when people note that they are lapsing into an addictive experience. Here, overcome by despair and guilt, many people give themselves over to their failure and continue to the end point of the cycle—excess or intoxication. In order to short circuit the addiction cycle, it is necessary to forestall this guilt and despair and the act of surrender to which it leads. A therapy program may do this by indicating to clients that they will slip, that lapses are both understandable and forgivable, and that a lapse should not be a cue to abandon what has been accomplished. In this way, the guilt that is itself a prod to seek the addictive experience is diminished.

The belief people are sometimes taught that *entering* the addiction cycle will invariably culminate in a total breakdown of self-control is the best insurance that one slip will indeed lead to self-demeaning excesses. The alternative to this view is one which says that people always have a choice, even after they have taken a sip, a puff, or a bite. A treatment program communicates this view by stressing that clients should think in terms of avoiding the *next* bite, puff, or sip. The techniques that have been taught are valuable *at any point* in the addiction cycle.

Imagining the rewards of nonaddition. Imagination can be a powerful factor in changing people's behavior. The task of altering addictive habits is often that of the obese man who regulates his eating for a time, but sees no immediate change in his appearance. If he can visualize in his mind the way he will look and feel after continued dieting, he may be able to repeatedly resist overeating until the image he sees in his mirror matches that of the thin, active human being he sees in his mind. On every day that addicted smokers don't smoke, they may be heartened by visualizing the healthy, uncongested individuals they will eventually be.

A variety of addiction-treatment techniques are based on creating a system of rewards contained entirely within people's minds. The most straightforward tactic is simply to urge people to be quick to compliment themselves on the progress they have made, to glow inwardly whenever they eat a sensible meal or avoid an unnecessary snack. It is also possible for people to use their imagination to influence their view of themselves. Instead of regarding themselves as weak and their cause as hopeless, people with addictions can practice thinking of themselves as if they already *were* the people they wanted to be. They may rehearse such thoughts as "I deserve to be treated well" or say to themselves in challenging situations "I can resist the impulse to ______."

Some therapists have given the philosophy behind these methods the modern-sounding name of *cognitive ecology.* Others see in them a reflection of the practices of Clifford Beers, the founder of the mental hygiene movement in the twenties, who repeated to himself, "In each and every way I'm getting better every day." Yet however we describe this approach to human change, the inward responses to stimuli that are our thoughts are real indicators of how we conceive of ourselves. And these self-conceptions are crucial factors in addiction.

Imagining negative reinforcements. The negative reinforcement most people think of in connection with behavior modification is electrical shock. Related aversive techniques are sometimes employed to discourage addictions. Antabuse, for example, is an aversive drug used with alcoholics. Its initial effect is to make the taste of alcohol abhorrent to the drinker. Later, when the person recalls the taste of alcohol, the memory of nausea in connection with it acts as a deterrent to further drinking. There is an old folk method that has much the same effect in the case of smoking. Frank Conroy describes in *Stop Time* how, when he was a student, a truck arrived with enough cigarettes for everyone in his school. Conroy was encouraged to smoke continuously until he became completely sick, after which he never smoked again.

Heavy aversive conditioning is far from infallible. In the first place, it does not cause addicts to deal with their desire for the addictive experience. Moreover, most people do not wish to submit themselves to aversive conditioning, since they find it unpleasant and degrading. It is possible, however, to carry out aversive conditioning without resorting to electric shocks or induced nausea. Less objectionable negative reinforcers may be employed whose effect is imagined rather than experienced concretely.

People in the throes of an addiction lose sight of the negative aspects of their habits. Their immediate need for an addictive experience blots out all other considerations. Addicted individuals can be taught to think of negative consequences at the same time that they feel a desire for the object of their addiction. One program shows alcoholics videotapes of themselves when they are intoxicated. Smokers can be taught to anticipate the harsh feeling in the back of the throat that comes from smoking too many cigarettes, or to envision unpalatable actions—such as licking a dirty ash tray—whenever they feel an urge to smoke.

It would seem, then, that any information about the harmful impact of smoking, drinking, and overeating would fuel people's negative imaginings about what will happen to them if they persist in unhealthy habits. To some extent this may be true. There has been, for example, a recent drop-off in smoking among certain sectors of the population along with more public health information about tobacco's deleterious effects. Generally speaking, however, human beings have a tremendous capacity for denying negative information. Heavy smokers, for instance, are very likely to ignore facts about how smoking is harming them.

Presenting the health hazards of an activity is most useful when people have *halted* the activity. In these cases, the information supports decisions that have already been made. Thus lectures on the organ damage done by alcohol or the extra work overweight causes for the heart will be most appreciated by people who have successfully begun the first stage of treatment. The fact that, at different stages, people can make use of different types of negative and positive reinforcement is illustrated by one woman who, after she first quit smoking, would sit close to smokers in order to get a whiff of their tobacco. After a year of abstinence, she felt good every time she saw a smoker light up because she had the thought that she was no longer hurting herself in this way.

Finding social models and rewards. Throughout this book we have emphasized the close connection between the group and the individual in regard to addiction. A person's social environment influences whether the person becomes addicted and what he or she becomes addicted to, it inspires moderation or excess, and it can be a powerful tool for modifying or eliminating habits. Social reinforcement may take the form of applause at a Weight Watchers meeting or simply encouragement from one's family and friends, or act as a negative reinforcement when those who count on a person react with disappointment when he or she falls back into old habits.

Thus, as we have seen, programs for the treatment of

addicted individuals often involve group support and rewards for the individual, either from people in similar situations or from those who are concerned with the person's well-being. More than this, the group of which the addicted person is part—or any group—may itself be the object of efforts to combat addiction. Finally, as we have also seen, a person who wishes to end an addiction may be forced to leave behind past associations, and even intimate relationships, in order to do so.

Planning and setting goals. A therapeutic program differs from a person's normal routines in that it has a specific aim; the person is striving to reach a goal. A first step for the person, then, is to set a goal or a series of goals, and to map out a plan—under the direction of the program—for reaching them. Embarking on the program requires that the person make a commitment to achieving his goals. One way of establishing such a commitment is to have the person bet on himself. For example, he may be asked to give a friend a certain amount of money that he will get back only if he reaches his goal. Nonprofit programs may offer to refund a person's tuition to create a similar kind of incentive.

To know when he has succeeded, the person will have to record both his goal and his progress toward it. A specific weight loss, a date for being "smoke-free," a week in which he has had only a set number of drinks, can all be noted as signposts of his progress. The achievement of intermediate steps to a goal becomes the person's weekly or monthly aim, and he discusses his success or failure regularly with his group or therapist.

Finding alternate activities. A person fighting addiction needs to seek out new relationships, groups, and activities that help him spend time in healthier ways. One type of activity in particular is often used in combating addictions—a method of managing stress. So much of addiction is a direct reaction to stress that many treatment programs teach meditation, biofeedback, self-hypnosis, or other relaxation techniques. The person is then instructed to use the method at home at regular intervals or whenever a stressful occurrence—one likely to cause him to go back to his addiction—looms. Ideally, the person will gradually become less self-conscious about resorting to the relaxation technique, and more able to organize and limit stress reactions as a normal part of his functioning.

Practicing stress-reduction techniques does not mean becoming a cult member. In fact, the more straightforward the technique and the less rigamarole it involves, the better it will fit into an overall treatment program. Deep muscle relaxation is probably the most basic—and least distracting—technique for controlling stress. There is little to be gained, however, by recommending one such method over any other. Physical exertion of any kind will produce important benefits while dissipating unwanted energy. Whatever the activity, in order for it to have a chance against an addiction, it must build a bridge from the world of deleterious habits to the rewards that can be gotten in the larger world. If a behaviorally oriented program—or any other program—does not keep this larger aim in sight, then it will bog down under the weight of its own techniques, however well these work in isolation.

9
Developing healthy habits

Encouraging healthy habits and discouraging addictions are not separate tasks. This becomes clear in therapies that replace addictions and unhealthy habits with activities as varied as meditation, praying, or running. For example, when Kenneth Cooper began his research on aerobics with military personnel, he quickly discovered that a regular regimen of running had repercussions in other areas of his subjects' lives. Many of the men, besides improving their aerobic performance, gave up smoking and drinking and lost weight.

The elimination of one habit as another is acquired is not due only to the fact that people don't have time for two activities. Cooper's subjects gave up smoking and drinking because these old habits were not consistent with the good feelings and positive self-image produced by running. Healthy habits reduce the lure of addictions because they enhance people's sense of themselves. One of the ways they do this is by making people feel that they are in control of their own health and well-being. Such a feeling is totally opposite to the sense of helplessness that is the basis of addiction.

issues in selecting habits

In America the promulgation of healthy habits has become an industry. Commercial organizations each promote their own brand of meditation; nonprofit but powerful and prestigious groups promote running as the key to well-being; classes in yoga, tai-chi, and a host of eastern philosophies abound. Masses of people seem constantly on the lookout for new sources of physical or spiritual vigor. Why do so many people, not all of them young, feel that they must look so far afield for rewarding activities? Is there nothing in their own lives that could grow into a substantial healthy habit?

Obviously, there is an appeal in a new involvement. There is what we might call the clean-slate phenomenon. If people feel somewhat polluted by their previous involvements, what better remedy is there than to take a course, get some new paraphernalia, and do something they have never before attempted? This time, they resolve, they will be able to concentrate and make real progress; this time they will not make the mistakes that ruined past activities.

Returning to old pursuits in search of healthy involvements has certain dangers. Often these activities are intimately associated with scenes and people that would be better left behind. For example, a man may feel uncomfortable about renewing the fishing trips he used to enjoy if, while on such trips, he always drank too much in the evening with his buddies. Old patterns always have a pull of their own, and in returning to them a person is more likely than not to repeat their unhealthy aspects.

On the other hand, new activities, however pristine their appeal, are—at least in the beginning—artificial. Taking lessons, joining a group, purchasing books, records, and equipment; all are indications that what people are doing is not in their normal repertoire of actions, and that they are seeking outside themselves for involvements they hope will be meaningful. This hope may or may not be fulfilled. There are surely more dropouts from every type of therapeutic group and activity than there are people who stick with it, especially after an initial period of enthusiasm. If an activity is not already ingrained in the currents of a person's life, then these currents must be modified to support the activity. The less compatible an activity is with a person's present way of life, the less likely it is that the activity will take hold.

refurbishing an old sport

Bob had been a varsity-level golfer at a small college. Since his early teens he had gotten great pleasure from playing golf on public links on sunny afternoons. In college, for the first time, he was in a competitive situation. Not only did his score *really* count for him, it affected his teammates as well. When the time came to play for the championship of the conference in which his college participated, Bob knew his team was superior. He also knew when he teed up on the first hole that he was going to play a mediocre game. He just hoped that his teammates would make up for his poor showing by playing exceptionally well. They didn't, and Bob's team went down to defeat.

After college Bob went to business school to study accounting. Upon graduation he was offered a chance to manage the financial side of a college friend's new business. Bob knew that his friend had a good chance of being a success. The friend had the ability and the energy to succeed, and the launching of the business was well-timed. Yet Bob chose instead to go to work for a stable, medium-sized company. Although his friend hadn't asked him to put his own money into the new company,

Bob felt much more secure going with an established business that offered him a guaranteed, if limited, future. Bob was married by now, but his wife earned her own salary, and his choice was more a reflection of a personal predilection than any special family needs.

Twelve years later, Bob was still with the same company. In the meantime, his friend's business had prospered. Bob saw that this man was able to live life on a grander scale than he was, but that did not trouble him unduly. What did bother Bob was a feeling that life had passed him by: that he had reached a plateau from which he would never escape, and that his life was destined to be mediocre. More troublesome than all this was his gradual realization that his original choice had been based on fear—a fear of the unknown and worse, a fear about how good he was.

Bob had continued to play golf on and off. He was a good duffer and could beat practically anybody he came in contact with through business or on vacation, or during chance encounters on the golf course. Bob now had two children and was in his late thirties. One day he was free to play golf, but he had no partner. Deciding to go out on his own, he picked up two partners at the course and they began a game. The day was beautiful and Bob was feeling especially good. At the twelfth hole, he was at par. It was the first time he had played this well since his early twenties.

Bob's partners had an odd, if perhaps predictable reaction. They were at first amazed to see him hit the ball so well. As the game progressed and the margin between their scores and Bob's increased, they became annoyed, even resentful. Perhaps it was his imagination, but Bob felt that they wanted him to play badly. As he teed up on the thirteenth hole, he imagined that their eyes were on his back. His drive went off the fairway. Strangely, when Bob played the last six holes miserably, his companions relaxed and joked about his performance, implying that it was the end and not the beginning of the match which typified his game.

At home that evening, Bob thought over what had occurred. How could he have been so easily rattled by two men whom he would never see again? As he mulled over the question, he began to see a connection between his performance on the golf course and the way he behaved in other situations, such as at work. He also remembered his failures as an athlete in college. On the other hand, he was exultant about how well he had played. After all, he mused, he did go two-thirds of a round playing better than he ever had. On the whole, the day rekindled in Bob feelings toward golf he hadn't had since his teens.

Because he realized that nothing else he did could compete with golf as a source of good feelings Bob decided to play more seriously. He arranged with his wife to have Sundays free to golf. Since there were a large number of courses within a fifty-mile radius of his home, he decided to select a different course for each Sunday's outing. He then began asking acquaintances, one each of his golfing and nongolfing friends, to accompany him when he played. Sometimes both parties would accept, and he would have an uneasy threesome of experienced and inexperienced golfers. It was easier when one of the two turned him down, and Bob could pitch his game to either the more expert level of a fellow golfer, or the rougher game of a novice.

When both his invitees turned him down, Bob was at first reluctant to continue with his plans. He had had enough bad experiences touring courses with the Sunday golfers in plaid pants he met by chance. Yet eventually he decided to stick to his scheduled game whenever the weather was good. More often than not he enjoyed the company of the people he met on the course. He even made plans to play again with several men he met this way.

Of course, the pleasure Bob derived from golf, though substantial, was not as intense as it had been when he was younger—it was for this reason that he spiced up each outing by choosing a new course and a variety of partners. On the other hand, some of the changes he had made in the way he approached the game pleased him. Bob, who had always been careful with money, for the first time in his life didn't flinch at paying a substantial fee to play at some private club he had selected. He also ceased spending half an hour looking for lost balls, as he had done when he was younger.

But what he liked most was getting out, driving someplace new, and experiencing the adventure and excitement of a game which might be challenging in some way. Bob had not again run into people like the two men who had intimidated him on that one occasion. Still, he looked forward to the times he was able to find a good, competitive game, and when he did he generally acquitted himself well. When winter came and he was forced to give up golf, Bob found that he missed it. But he also felt a sense of accomplishment—a sense of having brought something back into his life that was fun and that was good for him, and that he was able to do better than he had ever done before. That winter he also decided to begin looking for another job.

using healthy activities as therapy

Laura was a therapy client who came to me because of a problem in her relationship with Bill, the man she lived with. They had met when she was nineteen and still lived at home. They began living together when Laura's job caused her to be transferred to another city and Bill moved with her. This was the first time Laura had been away from her mother and sister upon whom she had been terribly dependent all her life.

Her anxiety attacks began when Bill stayed out all night.

Later, after their relationship had calmed down, Laura was not able to shake these attacks. They occurred when she had to take public transportation by herself (which she needed to do to get to and from work) and she would have to wait for Bill to pick her up at the station. While riding on the bus or train Laura would panic. Her heart palpitating and short of breath, she felt as if she would faint if she didn't get off quickly.

Laura saw several doctors and therapists. Yet she never felt she got the kind of help she needed from these sources. She did receive prescriptions for medication, and when she couldn't count on Bill's being around, she could take Valium. But she didn't want to continue taking the drug indefinitely. When she came to me, we began by exploring the history of her intimate relationships, including those with her mother, sister, and boyfriend. We discussed her ideas about herself and her attitudes toward her boyfriend and love relationships in general. We also discussed her legitimate gripes about Bill's behavior.

We both felt that Laura needed something she could do independently that she could feel good about and which would be tension reducing. The activity she selected was yoga, something she had been meaning to try for a long time. Laura was a solid worker, and she approached yoga lessons in the same systematic way she approached a task at work. She began looking for a yoga class near her home while laying the groundwork for Bill to accept her going out on her own. She didn't want Bill to resent her independence, which might drive him to display the kind of unreliable behavior that had upset her in the past. On the other hand, she wanted to indicate to him that she needed to take up some kind of satisfying activity for her personal well-being.

As Laura attended her classes and set aside time each day to practice her exercises and breathing, she got the good feelings she was seeking. The physical activity involved in yoga itself made her feel good. What's more, when going to classes she was able to travel alone without being overcome by anxiety. She was delighted when, on her way home from class one night, her car broke down and she experienced no anxiety. Her growing self-assurance generalized. When she was on public transportation now and she felt uneasy, she quickly concentrated on her breathing exercises. After a time, she no longer even felt the signs of panic when travelling on the train.

Laura's therapy involved more than finding a rewarding activity to participate in. Among other things, she also had to learn to cope with Bill's reactions to her, to her class, and to her independence. Still, her involvement in yoga was very important to the success of her therapy. Yoga for Laura was an important example of the benefits a new habit can have, and of the meaning of the term "healthy" habit.

reprise—what makes a healthy habit

What is it about Bob and Laura's involvements in these cases that made them healthy habits? First and foremost, each activity was linked to a thoughtful analysis both of the problem it was meant to solve and the role the activity was meant to fill. Bob and Laura selected golf and yoga for concrete reasons; both had goals that they expected the activities to help them achieve. In each case, the activity they selected enabled them to confront without anxiety dilemmas that had held them back in life. This was most obvious in the case of Laura, who urgently needed to address her panic states. Because yoga enabled her to control her reactions to stress, it allowed her to examine the destructive and limiting way in which she had heretofore related to men.

Since to all outward appearances Bob was already functioning in a satisfactory manner, the changes he underwent were less striking. But they were real nevertheless, and reflected personal growth in the face of a conflict that had troubled him for a long time. For the first time, he was able to do something about the fears of failure that caused him to be satisfied with less than the best in himself.

Both Bob's and Laura's healthy habits enabled them to grow, and this growth was evident in more than the realm of the habit alone. Each combined the mastery of an activity with an increased ability to cope with the world: Laura learned to be enough at peace with herself to *demand* fair treatment from her mate, and Bob became confident enough of his own reactions to put himself to the test in challenging situations.

What made their habits healthy was not just the impetus to growth that they provided, of course. The activities the two people chose to participate in were also fun for them. Part of this pleasurableness lay in the familiarity of a welcome endeavor; part came from the unfolding of the self within the activity. The desire to avoid killing what he enjoyed in golf through repetition led Bob to try new partners and new golf courses. Given the discomfort playing a game with strangers could cause Bob, it was a significant step for him to repudiate predictability and to play sometimes wherever and with whomever he might.

Engaged in a different kind of search, Laura at first simply appreciated the calm yoga enabled her to attain. Yoga was not something that really fit in with the person she was, however. It could not be a lifelong source of satisfaction. In part because she realized this—and in part because mastering yoga permitted her to take other steps—Laura decided to begin singing lessons. As a member of a schoolgirl choir, she had once dreamt of being a great singer; yet she had never developed her strong voice and sense of music. After six months of lessons, Laura once more joined a vocal ensemble, this time a local choir. It is not only activities that entail muscular exertion that produce healthy habits. The pleasant sense of tiredness Laura felt after a practice or concert, the knowledge that she was making a contribution, and the transcendence of her daily cares that came when she lost herself in the act of singing, all were no less reinvigorating than demanding physical endeavors.

One other thing—perhaps coincidental—worth noting about these cases is that in neither did the person join a movement that demanded some prescribed level of allegiance. Both Laura and Bob were simply looking to gain from another experience something their current lives did not provide. It is certainly possible that an organized group or therapy could offer a person similar benefits. What is essential for the ultimate healthfulness of any habit is that it helps the person find more satisfaction in life, rather than serving as the person's entire source of satisfaction.

10

Pressures that maintain—and destroy—healthy habits

While there are legions of people who join groups, purchase the paraphernalia required by an activity, and send away for membership cards, a large percentage of these people sooner or later leave their healthy involvements by the wayside. Many more people attend smoking clinics, Weight Watchers, or meetings of groups of alcoholics than end up permanently free of their addictions. By the same token, most people who exercise, meditate, participate in sensitivity training, jog, and so on are never able to make the activity they take up a comfortable part of their lives.

There are many good reasons for wanting to limit one's participation in such groups or activities. An involvement may lose its appeal or become unsuitable for a person; or he or she may have learned as much as possible from it and want to move on. This occurred in Laura's case in the previous chapter, and she proceeded from yoga to singing.

Unfortunately, when people quit a healthy activity, they often return to the excesses and unhealthiness that caused them to take up the activity in the first place. They find that unless they keep up—or accelerate—their commitment to the activity, they regress. There are actually two parts to this problem which we shall consider in this chapter. First, what factors affect people's adoption of a healthy habit and the likelihood that they will continue a program of self-improvement? Second, beyond this state, when and why do the factors attaching people to an activity become so overpowering that the balance which makes for health is upset?

social factors that affect the maintenance of healthy habits

Societal and cultural factors. When a whole society becomes health conscious, it is easier for any given individual to maintain healthy patterns of living. For example, if many people in an area run, the threshold for a person to try running is lowered. Indeed, after a critical point is reached, a person may begin to feel pressured *to* exercise. This state of affairs exists in our society, where the president and many other prominent Americans jog, where there is widespread publicity about the dangers of smoking, drinking, and eating the wrong food, and where the "quality of life" is often discussed. Yet, along with this apparent emphasis on health, we have overwhelming rates of obesity, heart disease, alcohol and drug abuse, and cancer.

For healthy habits to be ingrained in the lives of Americans, the *means* for carrying them out will have to be agreed upon and presented to people more consistently. One thinks of the Chinese, large groups of whom exercise together in factories and on farms, and for whom bicycles are a major means of transportation. In the United States, we have not even been able to agree on a national campaign against smoking. Similarly, drunk driving remains a major cause of death. Yet there are very few serious attempts nationwide to punish either the driver who drinks or the person who sells him alcohol.

Socioeconomic and ethnic background. To say that a society is health conscious or not health conscious is not strictly accurate, since there is considerable variation in attitudes across different groups within the society. One of the most important determinants of health consciousness is a person's socioeconomic and educational level. Surveys show that people who are better off financially and who have more education are more likely to be aware of good health habits and to practice them. Thus joggers more often come from the middle and upper middle class, and antismoking programs have had more impact on those with more education.

People in the middle and upper strata of society are more likely to have healthy habits for a number of reasons. They may have more time to devote to activities like exercise. Because they are better educated, they may be better informed about which activities are healthful and unhealthful. Also, participation in various programs, eating better foods, and other healthy practices may cost money. But the difference between social groups is due to more than differences in free time, information, and wealth. There is a body of literature which shows that the higher people's standing in society is, the more concerned they become about healthy habits. For example, people in lower socioeconomic groups tend to approach each opportunity to eat as though they are not sure when they will have another chance for a good meal. Even when a person has the means to guarantee that he need never go hungry, this kind of attitude may persist. At higher socioeconomic levels, people learn to moderate their eating. They have faith that there will always be enough, and they know that a moderate calorie intake is better for them. Although some groups see corpulence as a sign of prosperity, the upper class in twentieth-century America has long valued a fashionable thinness.

A similar situation exists with regard to exercise. To people whose parents were laborers, exercise as a spare-time activity may not make sense, even if they themselves now perform a job that does not consume many calories or exercise their cardiovascular system. People from higher socioeconomic backgrounds, on the other hand, are more likely to value the good feeling and better health that come from exercise as necessary components to life.

It goes without saying that all the statements above have numerous exceptions. Among some immigrant groups, such as Jews and Italians, where eating tends to have an emotional significance in families, there is a higher incidence of overweight than might be predicted from an analysis of people's socioeconomic status and education. (Both groups have lower than average rates of alcoholism, however.) But there are certainly a large number of Italian and Jewish people who stay trim (and a small number who do become alcoholics). Variations of some kind occur in any group. Nevertheless, it is necessary to take social and cultural backgrounds into account in considering people's proclivities in relation to health. In the United States, black Americans are more likely to smoke, to be addicted to narcotics or alcohol, and to suffer from hypertension and obesity. For a number of reasons, their position in society has made them more susceptible to a variety of unhealthy habits.

Peer groups. One way in which people are able to overcome the impact of ethnicity and other immutable characteristics is by *choosing* the people with whom they will associate. We can divide the groups to which people belong into two categories. On the one hand, there are groups organized for specific purposes—such as losing weight or getting more exercise. On the other hand, there are groups of people who naturally get together because they enjoy one another's company. For example, have you ever noticed at a party that people who either smoke or don't smoke tend to congregate together? People who don't smoke often like to be with other nonsmokers because they don't enjoy smelling the fumes from other people's cigarettes. Also, people whose values either exclude or permit smoking are drawn together by their shared attitudes toward health and related matters.

Advantages of groups. Whatever their motives for wishing to be in the company of others who practice healthy habits, people benefit tremendously from doing so. They have the example, stimulus, and support of those around them to assist them in their endeavors to be healthy themselves. The people they know will order and cook sensible meals, won't tempt them with cigarettes, alcohol, coffee, or other drugs, and will respond positively to their efforts to moderate their behavior. If they are striving to commence a new activity, their fellow group members will reinforce their commitment, both by providing regular opportunities for practicing the activity and by expecting them to keep working at it.

Groups whose purpose is the pursuit of a specific activity also offer a sense of identity to participants. Members feel that they are set apart, that they are developing an ability that deserves respect. The more important an activity is to a group, the more its members tend to associate their identities with the activity.

Informal, or associational, groups do not produce such concrete identities as those which come from being a member of a roadrunners club or a transactional analysis group. Yet there is a sense of identity that comes from thinking of oneself as a health-seeking person—as a member of a large, vaguely defined group of people who prefer healthy habits to deleterious ones. This kind of identity, while more diffuse and less easily labeled, may be the most durable and pervasive. For it results in a way of thinking about oneself that manifests itself, as a matter of course, in natural and daily choices of healthy alternatives and avoidance of those things that detract from a healthy life.

individual factors that affect the maintenance of healthy habits

Setting goals. In Chapter 8 we saw that therapy programs often require people to set specific goals, to record their progress, and to adhere to a regimen they create with the help of the group or program. Creating healthy habits also involves setting goals, taking small steps and noting one's improvements and acknowledging periodic or occasional problems and slippages in proceeding toward these goals.

We first approached the topic of what level of performance a person aspires to achieve in the section on fear of failure in Chapter 2. We noted then that some people require themselves to achieve only the easiest, most certain goals, while others aspire to aims so lofty that they are nearly impossible to attain. Both these extreme approaches to goal-setting stem from a desire to avoid seriously challenging oneself, and thus to avoid any chance of failure. The middle ground between over- and underaspiring is to set goals that involve a meaningful change in one's life but are still realistic. More than this, goals must be flexible. If a person achieves his initial aims more rapidly than he expected, he should consider moving on to new challenges.

Evaluating feedback. To know how much progress one is making toward one's goals, one must have some way of getting information about progress being made. This information is called *feedback,* and incorporating it into an assessment of one's goals completes the feedback *loop.* Programs to help people lose weight or stop smoking not only have goals that are fairly clear, but progress toward these goals is relatively easy to assess.

Some health-oriented activities share this concreteness in their standards; indeed, this may be one of running's greatest appeals. Anyone who takes the trouble to run several times a week will nearly always be able to see that he can run farther or faster very quickly. All a neophyte has to do to measure his improvement is to look at his watch or to count the number of times he goes around a track or a block of houses. Eventually a person may be able to run without timing herself or without knowing how much distance she has covered and still be satisfied with her performance. Such a person has developed her internal standards to such a degree that external indicators are not necessary.

Other activities do not produce such clear signs of advancement. How, for instance, does a person know he or she is improving at—or benefiting from—yoga? The same applies to activities like meditation and to all kinds of psychotherapy and consciousness groups, such as est or transactional analysis. Since these activities do not come with ready-made standards, a person involved in them must depend on subjective impressions or on observing other participants to determine how much he or she is gaining from the activity.

Unfortunately, subjective evaluations by people who have a stock in an activity entail predictable difficulties. A person has a natural desire to think his or her involvements are worthwhile. Moreover, others who are involved in the same activity—like a therapist, a group leader, or fellow group members—have a similar need to see their efforts as productive. Thus, regardless of whether any benefits are forthcoming from an activity, there are strong pressures for people to believe that benefits exist and to persuade others who are involved that this is the case. A novice, who is proportionally more dependent on the opinions of others, is frequently taught that an activity is valuable at the same time he or she is taught how to *perform* that activity. This indoctrination makes it even less likely that the newcomer will be able to assess the costs and benefits of the activity objectively.

The solution for a person who seeks genuine information about her progress is to look *outside* the involvement for signs that her life is improving. An important source of such information is people who care for the person but who are not themselves involved in the group or activity. If such people fail to see positive changes when the person believes these have taken place, she must evaluate this conflicting data carefully. In addition, the goals she sets for herself at the outset of the involvement should be as concrete as possible so that she can determine how well they are being met. Merely being told by others in the group that she is doing well and finding that she can act more like a veteran of the group is no guarantee of positive growth.

People often attend sensitivity groups or seek other forms of therapy to improve their relationships with people. If this is a person's goal, then he will want the number and quality of his relationships outside the group to improve as a result of his being part of the group. Any other goal can be similarly translated into more or less concrete terms, but the translation takes effort, as does monitoring one's life for indicators of progress or lack of progress. It might seem that anyone capable of making these efforts would be able to make positive changes without enlisting in a group or in therapy. This is, in fact, the case. Such people are also likely to gain the most from therapy.

Accepting progress or a lack of progress. How much progress is enough? Only a person seeking to change can answer this question. In doing so, however, he must take into account how much energy, money, and other resources he has expended for whatever results he has achieved. For a person who goes to an analyst every day for several years, the rewards should ultimately be substantial; and indeed many people in this situation claim that this is the case. If, on the other hand, a person has made more modest attempts to change, he may be more relaxed about what he expects from his efforts.

Paradoxically, it is sometimes from more limited endeavors that the most clearcut gains come. An older person who has decided to take a walk every evening to improve her health or the way she sleeps can nearly always determine whether she is getting the benefits she wishes from her investment in exercise. More ambitious therapies are more risky enterprises. There are significant numbers of people who have tried some form of psychotherapy who feel that their efforts were wasted, or even that the results were detrimental. Even when people feel that they have benefited from psychotherapy, improvements in their "mental health," "psychological functioning," or "self-actualization" may be difficult for others to perceive.

In any activity, small gains are easier to realize and may be more satisfactory than grandiose ones. For example, suppose a person does sit-ups several times a week. If he is content to stay at one level, improving very gradually over a long period, the benefits of the exercise will be small but distinct. If, on the other hand, he tries to up the number of sit-ups he does each day and fails, he may quit in discouragement. For many people, the simple act of performing a physical activity makes them feel sufficiently healthy to warrant a small investment of time. More demanding regimens, while appropriate for some, can have the disastrous effect for others of bringing about failure and avoidance of the activity altogether.

Failing to achieve goals is probably what scuttles most people's attempts to improve themselves. Yet it is rare for progress along any path to be uninterrupted. If a person is forced to miss one session of exercise or meditation, one violin lesson or class, how will he react? While he may not intend this first lapse to be the beginning of the end, the resulting loss of impetus and resolution is often fatal. Just as most diets cease the first time the person overeats, so most exercise programs end when the first injury or strain causes the person to drop out for a week or two. Just as in the case of diet or efforts to quit smoking, a person must accept and overcome interruptions in a self-imposed program in order to reorient his or her life.

Backsliding is normal. So are intentional or accidental hiatuses. Even the most successful practitioner of an activity encounters plateaus in progress. The first flush of improvement is a stimulus to continued efforts, but there is always a point at which further inputs do not lead as dependably to greater results. The person has reached what is for him, at least for a time, his natural level. He may be satisfied to continue indefinitely at this stage, or he may decide to try harder to reach a higher level. Or eventually he may conclude that he would be better off spending his time doing something else. All these choices, and others not mentioned, are reasonable ones—so long as they are made with an appreciation of one's own powers and limitations. Healthy choices are *not* made if a person's self-respect is undermined by the knowledge that progress is never unlimited, that change can be difficult, and that it often is subject to fits and starts.

from healthy to unhealthy—the road to excess

It is part of the human condition that the same factors which support healthy habits can drive people to unhealthy excesses. There are unhealthy levels of commitment to an involvement that make it indistinguishable from an addiction, however healthy it was at the start. The following variables, which define excessive involvement, derive from the criteria for addiction put forward in this book.

The desire for an ultimate solution. All people have moments when they wish that a problem would disappear, or that a simple solution existed for whatever was bothering them. There are industries based on this desire in the health field. Popularizers of fad diets and makers of diet pills and machines that promise to "make pounds melt away" have made fortunes from such fantasies. One woman told me that she daydreamed of a machine she could hook up to her body that would give her all the daily exercise she needed.

Some people feel the need to simplify their lives more strongly than others. They want to have their problems totally resolved with little or no effort on their part. Such wishes are, indeed, characteristic of the addicted person, who finds life's complexity a strain with which he is unable to cope. The same wish for magical solutions may be found in some of those who pursue various therapeutic involvements. These people want to believe that if they join a movement, or follow completely the instructions of a certain group, they need do nothing more to ensure their psychological or physical health. They may believe that their "healthy" commitment excuses a multitude of sins and will compensate for any number of unhealthy transgressions they commit. This kind of attitude is frequently characteristic of a person's approach to all experience. Often fervent exponents of one activity have histories of excessive behavior, as did Jim, the runner in Chapter 4.

Dependence on one activity for a desired effect. One man, an accountant, was treated by a number of leading therapists over a period of eighteen years. At the end of that time, he appeared no better able to function than he had been at the beginning of his treatment. This man reported that he felt free of anxiety only during his therapy sessions, when he engaged in free association or some other interaction with his therapist. In these circumstances, an addiction exists. The person is only able to achieve the experience he seeks in a single setting—the therapist's office—to which he must constantly return.

Any tension-reducing activity as well as therapy can have this addictive effect. In biofeedback programs where a person learns to relax at the sight of a particular cue, say a restful picture, the aim is to enhance the person's ability to relax anywhere. If the person only feels relaxed in front of this cue, he has actually become wedded to the training program, the room in which he relaxes, and the picture. Like someone who must take tranquilizers to maintain his or her equilibrium, the person has not developed his emotional and coping capacities so as to function with less stress. He therefore becomes addicted to the biofeedback training.

One young woman who had been tense all her life got a job recording prescriptions at a hospital pharmacy. At times the pressures on her became especially frenetic, and she would explode angrily at those around her. She then began a meditation program. She enjoyed meditating, found it helpful, and was good at it. However, she was still rarely without tension at work or whenever she was not meditating. Eventually she began to take several meditation breaks during the day. Because it was impossible to tell when demands for prescriptions at the hospital would jump, she missed several peak periods at the pharmacy and was fired from her job.

At this time the woman was offered an opportunity to pay her own way to attend a training institute in Europe that would qualify her as a meditation instructor. She eventually worked in this capacity, and although she earned less than she had at the hospital, she found her new life far less stressful. But this did not mean that she left behind the temper tantrums for which she had been known at the hospital. When her husband—who meditated also but did not make a profession of it—asked her to do things she feared would interfere with her periods of meditation, she lashed out at him in rage. He grew into the habit of protecting her from such demands, and of excusing her outbursts to friends who observed them by telling them she was having "a stress attack."

Did this woman learn to dissipate tension through meditating? Only in a limited way. When it came to carrying out important obligations to her husband and to nonmeditators, her behavior showed no improvement. Since meditation did not affect her disposition toward her environment *aside* from that involvement, she was forced to turn increasingly to it as her chief means of achieving satisfaction. In this sense the activity was effective. However, from the standpoint of the health of her relationship to the world at large, meditation was harmful, and growing increasingly so.

Addiction to a group. Groups have lives of their own. People gain satisfactions from belonging to a group that have nothing to do with the stated purpose of the group. Sometimes these satisfactions become wholly independent of—and may even run counter to—the group's official aims.

We have noted that group support is often desirable and necessary for people trying to change. But appreciation of the group can extend far beyond its demonstrated effectiveness. A person may come to see a group's values and ideals as so superior that membership in the group becomes her principal criterion for accepting another person. When this happens, she ceases to evaluate what she is gaining from membership in the group—such as peace of mind, health, or a better ability to navigate life. If she were still concerned about such things, she would encounter and accept many people who achieved them in other ways. Instead, the addicted group member denies that anyone who does not share her group affiliation can possess these virtues.

The identity the group buttresses for the individual then grows to be entirely a group identity. It is maintained by subscription to the group's values and beliefs, consistent identification of oneself as a group member, defense of the group in the face of questioning and opposition from others, and a prejudice against everything and everyone not connected with the group. The more tightly a person adheres to a group identity, the more likely the person is to invite a negative reaction from others. This negative reaction prompts the person to exhibit greater defensiveness and to identify further with the group. Thus his life becomes more and more constricted.

the opposite of addiction—balance

The stresses involved in maintaining healthy habits—especially when they are new or incompatible with former habits or when they are adopted by someone who is not good at keeping to the middle ground in personal matters—can quickly push a person to the point where beneficial results are replaced by damaging ones. This occurs when an activity and its decorative concomitants become more important than the healthy aims the activity was supposed to produce.

For a healthy habit to become established, it must become important enough in a person's life so that it will not be discarded for trivial reasons. A person must make a pact with himself to perform the activity with sufficient frequency that he is doing more than paying lip service to it. But when this entails losing sight of and denigrating other activities—many of which have other benefits—tbe first step has been taken on the path toward addiction. The repetition of one way of health will always pass a point beyond which its rewards diminish, while the rewards from unexplored activities increase proportionally. Knowing when this point is reached is the key to achieving a balanced life.

11

The nonaddicted lifestyle:

balance and proportion

If it is true that a crucial element in a healthy lifestyle is the ability to vary our choices, to shift our preferences as circumstances dictate, and to subjugate any individual activity to an overall goal of healthfulness, then it is as important for us to know how to control an involvement as to encourage it. Oddly enough, one of our major sources of information about how to do this is the literature on drug abuse which examines the characteristics of people who use illicit drugs in moderation. Norman Zinberg, Charles Winick, Irving Lukoff, and others have uncovered groups of people who employ the most potent pharmacological agents—including narcotics—without allowing the drugs to disrupt their lives. What factors allow such people to control their use of drugs while others become enslaved to chemicals? Answers to this question are relevant to all of us who seek to be the masters of our involvements rather than their slaves.

maintaining other interests

Not going overboard with a fresh activity is difficult when there is nothing else of substantial interest in life to provide us with ballast. Thus, while we may feel so inspired by a new endeavor that we wish to throw over everything else, we are not serving ourselves well by doing so. A first step to introducing changes in our lives is to assess what we have that is valuable. Perhaps many of our previous commitments, pursuits, and associations are limited; but in noting their limitations we are doing nothing more than acknowledging the conditions of life.

We have self-respect when we realize that, while we are not perfect, what we have done up to any point in our history is an expression of ourselves worth acknowledging. There are two strands of our lives that should never be ignored in this regard—our intimate relationships and the work we do. When these do not seem worth continuing in the face of some promising new venture, then we need first to consider what problems we are having with them. For to reject our work and our relationships is to repudiate who we are, generally for benefits that may be temporary at best. What can be most healthy about some new activity is the increased ability it gives us to sort out our relationships and to accept—or change—the conditions of our work.

having moderate expectations

If something seems so good to us that we believe it will solve all our problems, then we ought not yet to become involved in it. We need to think about exactly what we want from a therapy, a group, an exercise program, a spiritual movement, or an activity—and then imagine how we would benefit from having our wants met. We cannot lose sight, however, of the fact that benefits are proportional to the work done to achieve them. In health as in economics, there are no free lunches.

choosing appropriate alternatives

The ability to choose alternatives—and to be sated with one activity and then to cease it—is such an important key to healthy habits that it can be the basis of a regular "health check." This check can take the form of any of a series of related questions about any activity, whether it be meditating, running, belonging to Weight Watchers, est, or AA, being in therapy, or sky diving: "Can I grow tired of this activity?" "Is there anything I can gain from some other activity that I don't gain from this one?" "Can I enjoy myself on a day when I don't do this?" When the answer to any or all of these questions is no, then the arrow points to addiction. The best way to exercise our ability to choose what we will do is by delaying, omitting, replacing, or changing an activity. In other words, we must occasionally say yes to some alternative if we are to believe that we are free to do so. We can even look forward to trying something different to see whether we might like to do it regularly. Incidentally, the question to ask others in order to discover if we can rely on their description of the benefits of an activity is, "What is the biggest drawback you see to doing this?" If they say there is none, their opinion cannot be trusted.

having friends with a variety of interests

It is a mistake to demand as a badge of friendship that others share our preoccupations, or even all our interests. True, friends are people with whom we have significant things in common. But we cannot gain a perspective on our endeavors from mirror images of our own views. Knowing people who do different things for fun, for health, for exercise, for meaning, may not make us want to partake of all these things ourselves. But having such friends will certainly help us to round out our awareness of the variety life has to offer. They are also the best protection against being trapped into thinking that our way to health is the only way.

It is not possible for most of us to taste all the variety there is in life. Yet there are people who participate seriously in a broad range of healthy activities. Knowing about such people can benefit us just as having models of moderate drug use is the best guarantee that children will not become drug abusers.

pulling it all together

Jane Brody, a writer on scientific and health topics for *The New York Times,* outlined her personal philosophy of exercise and diet, of health, enjoyment, work, and feeling good in one of her columns. We reprint it here as an example of a balanced approach to healthfulness.

You will live long and enjoy life.

I know full well that this paper prophecy, which I found in a fortune cookie the other day, comes with no money-back guarantee for a good or long life. But while many people are content to accept whatever fate life may have in store, in the 15 years I have been a medical and science writer, I have come to believe that I can and should adopt reasonable measures to help preserve my health and prolong my life.

I know that the measures are no guarantee that I will still be spry at 90. I also know that many of the recommendations are based on a still-incomplete understanding of the major killing and crippling diseases. Some, in fact, may turn out to be wrong.

But I am convinced that my future health largely depends on how I care for myself in the present, and I try to live in accordance with what I consider the best available medical knowledge. It isn't always simple, but I have discovered that, contrary to what some people might think, it's not a life of misery and deprivation.

First, I want to respond to some of the more frequent comments of those who meet me or write to me: I am not too young to worry about my health. I'll be 38 this spring, and, anyway, I think it is never too early to start taking care of yourself. I am not thin by nature but by design and constant vigilance. I like to eat and, guided by reason and self-control, I eat everything I like. I exercise daily, even though my workday is regularly 10 to 12 hours long—I make time for the things I consider important. And, most important of all, I enjoy my life.

My guiding principle is moderation. Except for an absolute ban on smoking, I am not a fanatic about anything, unless you think it fanatic that I am determined to try to realize the prophecy in my fortune cookie. Now for the details:

Weight control. I once weighed a third more than I do now. I was always on a diet, and after a week of eating library paste and toothpicks, my willpower would run out and I'd gorge on everything I loved and had missed all week. Or else I would put nothing in my mouth all day, then eat nonstop all night. Eventually, I became obsessed with food and weight, and the more obsessed I was, the fatter I got.

Then one day I realized that I had to learn to live more sensibly with food. I stopped dieting and started eating like a normal person, three reasonable meals a day. No more binges, no more whole bags of potato chips or pints of ice cream and no more going hungry. And, lo and behold, I lost weight. It took two years to reach what I consider a normal weight for my size and bone structure, but I never gained it back. Here's how I do it:

I never skip a meal. That only makes me hungrier for the next meal and increases the likelihood that I'll overeat. Besides, when I'm hungry I'm irritable and impatient and I can't write. I consider breakfast and lunch my most important meals; they provide me with the energy I need to work productively and run around all day. I usually consume two-thirds or more of my day's calories by 2 P.M., just the reverse of what most others I know do.

If I've had a big lunch, I eat only a salad and a piece of bread for supper (then I often eat the leftover supper for breakfast the next day). If I've had only a sandwich for lunch, I eat a small portion of the family dinner plus the salad. If we're planning to have a big dinner out, I have a large breakfast and small lunch.

I don't consume much alcohol—at a dinner party, one drink plus wine with dinner; at home, a small glass of wine with supper. I find that in addition to the calories in alcohol, it diminishes my willpower, and I tend to overeat if I overdrink.

I must admit, though, that I have a sweet tooth (diminishing in intensity as I age). I keep it pretty well under control by allowing myself one or two sweets a day, usually two cookies and a slice of homemade sweet bread (for example, pumpkin, cranberry, zucchini or banana bread).

In a restaurant, I usually have fruit for dessert; in someone else's house, I'll eat a sliver of the pie or cake that's served. Ice cream, a lifelong passion, is consumed by the tablespoon instead of the scoop and only flavors I find irresistible; that way I don't feel deprived.

I weigh myself every day, sometimes twice. My weight usually fluctuates within a three-to-four-pound range. As soon as I hit the top of that range, I increase my vigilance. But I don't cut out, just down.

Exercise. When an injury kept me bedridden for six weeks last year, I discovered that I could, through determination, keep my weight down even without any exercise. But I have a lot more leeway in my diet when I'm active. Currently I swim a quarter-mile three times a week, jog two miles three times a week, play tennis one to five times a week (depending on the season), ride my bike often and walk lots. Whenever possible, I use footpower instead of cars, taxis, subways, busses, elevators and escalators.

This activity adds far more to my life than the few hundred extra calories I can eat each day. It is a great tension reliever and relaxant. I find that I get angry and frustrated less often and get over my destructive feelings more quickly than I used to when I exercised less regularly. And I sleep like a baby—about six hours a night—even though I always have a lot on my mind.

In sum, then, unless you have a chronic illness like diabetes or are genetically prone to an early death from heart disease, you need not become an extremist or an ascetic, nor do you have to give up everything you love forever, to live healthfully and enjoyably. Through the principles of moderation, you can have your cake and eat it too. All you have to do is decide it's something you want to do.

It is true that Ms. Brody differs from the average person in that she is a professional writer about medical and scientific topics, and has perhaps more freedom to arrange her life according to the principles she deems to be healthy. On the other hand, she does put in a long workday and is wife and mother to a family of four, so that her primary concerns are not different from the average person's. She is also not inherently "good." She has had a weight problem for much of her life and, like many of us, she spent a good deal of time worrying about her weight and dieting, and then giving in to her impulses and splurging. She does not seem to have had a problem with alcohol or drugs, and we cannot know about her other involvements. But hers seems to be a lifestyle she has chosen and evolved for herself, rather than one that was inborn. I think most of us can identify with the human being behind the article.

To achieve health, she has not become a devotee of any cult, movement, type of diet or exercise, or any other organized approach to living, playing, or being healthy. In fact, her approach to health is marked by its individuality and eclecticism. She is like most people in that she prefers to play a game such as tennis to stay fit rather than to pursue the solitary rituals of running and swimming. Yet when time or weather or other conditions don't permit her to play a game, she exercises systematically on her own. The personal regimens she follows are not excessively stern, and the quarter-mile of swimming or the two miles of running are well below what most devoted advocates of either of these activities would do. She is also as physically active within the normal routines of her business and family life as she can be.

Ms. Brody's life is a constant series of adjustments designed to keep it in balance. Most of these adjustments come almost as second nature to her now. They are not wrenching decisions that demand excruciating effort and self-sacrifice. When she gets exercise through one means she doesn't need to do as much of another physical activity. When she eats more than usual at one meal, she cuts down at another. She does allow herself treats, especially when something *special* is involved. By sampling a small slice of a host's dessert, she participates in a group activity while remaining true to her own values. At the same time she does not call undue attention to her divergent style of eating or offend those who extend themselves to her but whose habits differ from hers.

It is her ability to respond to sensations from her body that tells her when she needs to exercise and when she is weary. In controlling her weight, however, she needs assistance, and she relies on the mechanical aid of a scale to tell her how well she is doing. By using it frequently she knows right away when her weight is rising, and does not need to react drastically. Instead she cuts back mildly on her caloric intake.

The feelings and beliefs that underlie Ms. Brody's personal system are expressed at the beginning of her article, when she asserts that her health is something she controls. In her view, what she does on a daily basis will affect both the length and quality of the life that stretches before her, and the degree of contentment and good feeling she will experience through living. What's more, she has developed the confidence to tackle the far from easy task of reining in impulses and altering habits built up over a lifetime. She has done something about the factors that determine her health—she has changed habits that were hurting her, and nurtured others more compatible with her desire for a long and healthy life.

She has exceptions to all her rules, and her health practices overlap and interact in such a way that no one of them is dominant. In fact, this is the surest guarantee that her habits will remain healthy, and forever outside the realm of addiction. What Ms. Brody has is an *integrated* approach to life and health, one that involves all facets of her social, physical, and emotional self, and one that is true to her values and needs, and thus to the person she is.

is there a solution for addiction?

As individuals and as a society, we are struggling to free ourselves from addictive impulses. In attempting to do so, we often become confused about what it is we are striking out at and what it is we need in our lives. Unfortunately, these things cannot be listed for us, with one column headed "good activities" and the other "bad." It can be distressing to discover that addiction is not limited to a few illegal drugs, and that we cannot always clearly label what is an addiction and what is not. Even the things we introduce as cures for addictions often turn out to be themselves addictive.

But yes, there are addictions, as surely as there are healthy involvements. Our journey in this book has taken us to the point of observing that people who incorporate healthy habits into their lives find their awareness of themselves and their worlds enhanced. Their involvements with people and activities aside from those connected to their habits become happier. Their self-esteem is buoyed by more than temporary highs. They welcome change, expansion, and variation in their activities and relationships, and they derive from them much more than a temporary escape from unpleasantness in the rest of their lives.

In assessing what there is about a habit that makes it healthy, we must look as carefully at the person performing the activity as we do at the activity itself. Many of our impulses toward healthfulness are conditioned by our experiences in childhood. At the same time, our social environments contain powerful forces that can both retard and nurture healthy impulses. At the most basic levels, then, addiction is a political and cultural issue.

We can control social forces to the extent that we can choose the groups to which we belong and the people with whom we associate. Our involvements with people can inspire health. They can also become small worlds which narrow our lives rather than expand them. As we have seen, if we become so fixed in our pursuit of any one thing that we compulsively reject all other options in life, and all the people connected with these options, we have lost the essential elements which distinguish healthy habits from destructive addictions.

None of us is entirely free of addictive tendencies, just as no one is irretrievably trapped by addictive inclinations. If there were not a range of behavior of which all of us are capable, there would have been no reason for this book. In the realm of habits, a host of mechanisms has evolved for relearning how to relate to the world in a nondestructive way. All are based on nothing more than our own ability to note how much something is hurting us and how much we would gain by giving it up. While there are gimmicks that make the positive and negative consequences of our behavior more salient for us, they must be utilized in concert with an entire rethinking of our relationship to the world.

The social-psychological approach to addiction tells us above all that we need to find regular rewards in our everyday lives in order to follow a path of health. I am neither pessimistic nor optimistic about the prospects that any individual (including myself) or society as a whole will accomplish this. What I do know is that there is no short route to healthfulness. We can reach it only by developing competence, finding satisfaction, and defeating fear.

Sources and further readings

Chapter 1

Goldstein, Avram; Kaizer, Sophia; & Whitby, Owen. "Psychotropic Effects of Caffeine in Man," *Clinical Pharmacology and Therapeutics* 10 (1969): 477–497.

Leventhal, Howard; & Cleary, Paul D. "Why Haven't More People Quit Smoking?" *The Sciences* (November 1977): 12–18.

Peele, Stanton. "Redefining Addiction I: Making Addiction a Scientifically and Socially Useful Concept," *International Journal of Health Services* 7 (1977): 103–24.

Peele, Stanton, "Redefining Addiction II: The Meaning of Addiction in Our Lives," *Journal of Psychedelic Drugs* 11 (1979): 289–97.

Peele, Stanton; with Brodsky, Archie. *Love and Addiction.* New York: Signet, 1976.

Schachter, Stanley. "Pharmacological and Psychological Determinants of Smoking," *Annals of Internal Medicine* 88 (1978): 104–14.

Chapter 2

Atkinson, John W.; & Feather, Norman T., eds. *A Theory of Achievement Motivation.* New York: Wiley, 1966.

Becker, Howard S. *Outsiders.* London: Free Press of Glencoe, 1963.

Blum, Richard H.; & assoc. *Drugs I: Society and Drugs.* San Francisco: Jossey-Bass, 1969.

Chein, Isidor; Gerard, Donald L.; Lee, Robert S.; & Rosenfeld, Eva. *The Road to H.* New York: Basic Books, 1964.

Jessor, Richard; Young, H. Boutourline; Young, Elizabeth B.; & Tesi, Gino. "Perceived Opportunity, Alienation, and Drinking Behavior Among Italian and American Youth," *Journal of Personality and Social Psychology* 15 (1970): 215–22.

McClelland, David C.; Davis, William N.; Kalin, Rudolf; & Wanner, Eric. *The Drinking Man.* New York: Free Press, 1972.

Robins, Lee N.; Davis, Darlene H.; & Goodwin, Donald W. "Drug Use by U.S. Army Enlisted Men in Vietnam: A Follow-Up on Their Return Home," *American Journal of Epidemiology* 99 (1974): 235–49.

Winick, Charles. "Maturing Out of Narcotic Addiction," *Bulletin on Narcotics* 14 (1962): 1–7.

Zinberg, Norman E. "G.I.'s and O.J.'s in Vietnam," *New York Times Magazine* (December 5, 1971): 112–24.

Chapter 3

Armor, David J.; Polich, J. Michael; & Stambul, Harriet B. *Alcoholism and Treatment.* New York: Wiley, 1978.

Davies, David L. "Definitional Issues in Alcoholism." In Tarter, Ralph E. & Sugerman, Arthur A., eds. *Alcoholism.* Reading, Mass.: Addison-Wesley, 1976.

Dielman, T. E. "Gambling: A Social Problem?" *Journal of Social Issues* (Summer 1979): 36–42.

Livingston, Jay. *Compulsive Gamblers.* New York: Harper & Row, 1974.

Oates, Wayne. *Confessions of a Workaholic.* New York: World, 1971.

Pomerleau, Ovide; Pertschuk, Michael; & Stinnett, James. "A Critical Examination of Some Current Assumptions in the Treatment of Alcoholism," *Journal of Studies on Alcohol* 37 (1976): 849–67.

Rosenblatt, Paul C.; & Cunningham, Michael R. "Television Watching and Family Tensions," *Journal of Marriage and the Family* (February 1976): 105–11.

Winn, Marie. *The Plug-in Drug.* New York: Grossman, 1977.

Chapter 4

Glasser, William. *Positive Addiction.* New York: Harper & Row, 1976.

Kostrubala, Thaddeus. *The Joy of Running.* New York: Pocket Books, 1977.

Morgan, William P. "Negative Addiction in Runners," *The Physician and Sportsmedicine* (February 1979): 55–70.

Paffenbarger, Ralph S., Jr.; Wing, Alvin L.; & Hyde, Robert T. "Physical Activity as an Index of Heart Attack Risk in College Alumni," *American Journal of Epidemiology* 108 (1978): 161–75.

Peele, Stanton. Review of *Positive Addiction* in *Psychology Today* (April 1976): 36.

Pollock, Michael L.; & assoc. "Effects of Frequency and Duration of Training on Attrition and Incidence of Injury," *Medicine and Science in Sports* 9 (1977): 31–36.

Chapter 5

Kubie, Lawrence S. *Neurotic Distortion of the Creative Process*. Lawrence: University of Kansas Press, 1958.

Morgan, William P. "The Mind of the Marathoner," *Psychology Today* (April 1978): 38–49.

Chapter 6

Low, Ken. *Can Do: Building a Sense of Personal Effectiveness*. Calgary, Alberta: Calgary Board of Education, 1979.

Schachter, Stanley. "Obesity and Eating," *Science* 161 (1968): 751–56.

White, Burton L.; Kaban, Barbara T.; & Attanucci, Jane S. *The Origins of Human Competence*. Lexington, Mass.: Heath, 1979.

Wilkinson, Rupert. *Prevention of Drinking Problems: Alcohol Control and Cultural Influences*. New York: Oxford University Press, 1970.

Chapter 7

Allen, Robert; & Linde, Shirley. *Life Gain: A Culture-Based Approach to Positive Health*. Morristown, N.J.: Human Resources Institute, 1980.

Dole, Vincent P.; & Nyswander, Marie E. "Methadone Maintenance Treatment: A Ten-Year Perspective," *Journal of the American Medical Association* 235 (1976): 2117–19.

Lennard, Henry L.; Epstein, Leon J.; & Rosenthal, Mitchell S. "The Methadone Illusion." *Science* 176 (1972): 881–84.

Chapter 8

Enelow, Allen J.; & Henderson, Judith B., eds. *Applying Behavioral Science to Cardiovascular Risk*. Washington, D.C.: American Heart Association, 1975.

Gilbert, R. M. "Drug Abuse as Excessive Behavior," *Canadian Psychological Review* 17 (1976): 231–40.

NIDA. *Research Monograph Series 25: Behavioral Analysis and Treatment of Substance Abuse*. Washington, D.C.: U.S. Government Printing Office, 1979.

Polich, J. Michael; Armor, David J.; & Braiker, Harriet B. *The Course of Alcoholism: Four Years After Treatment*. Santa Monica, Cal.: Rand Corporation, 1980.

Pomerleau, Ovide; Pertschuk, Michael; & Stinnett, James. "A Critical Examination of Some Current Assumptions in the Treatment of Alcoholism," *Journal of Studies on Alcohol* 37 (1976): 849–67.

Vogler, Roger E.; Weissbach, Theodore A.; Compton, John V.; & Martin, G. T. "Integrated Behavior Change Techniques for Problem Drinkers in the Community," *Journal of Consulting and Clinical Psychology* 45 (1977): 267–79.

Chapter 9

Cooper, Kenneth H. *Aerobics*. New York: M. Evans, 1968.

Chapter 10

Becker, Marshall H., ed. *The Health Belief Model and Personal Health Behavior*. Thorofare, N.J.: Charles B. Slack, 1974.

Lieberman, Morton A.; Yalom, Irvin D.; & Miles, Matthew B. *Encounter Groups: First Facts*. New York: Basic Books, 1973.

Peele, Stanton. *Life-Sized Therapy: Putting the Therapy Experience in Perspective*. New York: New American Library, 1981.

Chapter 11

Jacobson, Richard; & Zinberg, Norman E. *The Social Basis of Drug Abuse Prevention*. Washington D.C.: Drug Abuse Council, 1975.

Lukoff, Irving F.; & Brook, Judith S. "A Sociocultural Exploration of Reported Heroin Use." In Winick, Charles, ed. *Sociological Aspects of Drug Dependence*. Cleveland, Ohio: CRC Press, 1974.

Winick, Charles. "Physician Narcotic Addicts," *Social Problems* 9 (1961): 174–86.

Index